M000318321

Enjoy My Book!

Monk vs. Monkey Mind

Becoming Aware of Your Thoughts to Manifest the Life of Your Dreams

Tzachi Ozeri

Monk vs. Monkey Mind

Becoming Aware of Your Thoughts to
Manifest the Life of Your Dreams

First Edition: 2023

ISBN: 9781524318468
ISBN eBook: 9781524328740

© of the text:
  Tzachi Ozeri

© Layout, design and production of this
edition: 2023 EBL

Table of Contents

MONK VS THE MONKEY MIND - WHO ARE YOU FEEDING?

Becoming aware of your thoughts to manifest the life your Dreams

Are you feeding the Monkey in your mind? Or the Monk? I think most of you clever cats know by now that when you think in a negative way (I like to call this the Monkey mind), you will attract Monkey results! Under the law of attraction, whatever you feed, gets bigger. Wherever you put your focus, that's what you'll see more of in your life.

You see, manifesting good things can be beautiful, oh, so beautiful! But you can just as easily manifest bad things and then wonder why you're always so unlucky.

I want to help you guys become more aware of the Monkey taking over your minds (he's loud!) and instead learn to listen to your wise, loving (but soft-spoken) Monk. He knows you. He knows what you need. He's got your back! You just must listen to him because if you don't, that Monkey, man, he'll take over like a mother...KER!

What we nurture, grows. What we manifest, happens. I see manifesting like going to the gym. You don't want to go, but you push yourself to. Once there, you push yourself to lift weights and run on the treadmill. Everything is so tough at first, and it makes you want to quit, right? It gets worse when you've been sweating it out 3 - 5 times a week and don't see any results straight away. What's the point?

The wonderful feeling after each workout, the satisfaction of working towards your goals which makes you continue, the relief mixed with the energy that comes from giving yourself a chance to know that it'll pay off in the end.

So, whatever challenges you're dealing with in life, you've got to stop feeding those initial negative thoughts (that Monkey!). Stop feeling sorry for yourself, stop indulging your doubts and laziness, and turn it into a positive.

And who is right with you, helping you to stop feeding the Monkey? Your Monk. Listen to him. Feel his love! He's saying, "You can do it. You got this!"

As soon as you begin to hear his dear voice, you are more aware of your energy, and you see the muscles you've worked on *have* changed. At this point, you get a burst of energy from *seeing* results. It becomes a self-perpetuating cycle because you're motivated to get better at what you're doing, achieving more, becoming more efficient, etc. You may even research ways to improve.

Once you get to the stage where you are happy and fulfilled, you may want to share it with those around you, or even help those in need. Perhaps just like someone did for you when they encouraged you to start going to the gym!

THAT'S HOW MANIFESTING WORKS! It's truly a beautiful thing which just attracts more and more fulfillment and happiness. Your Monk is behind all of this, and it's proof you have been listening to his soft yet powerful voice. It's proof you've been ignoring the loudmouth Monkey and letting your Monk's voice shine through. Not easy but *so* worth it!

Just like going to the gym, manifesting is a process which takes time to deliver results. (Although sometimes you can be surprised at just how quickly those results come.)

You might not see results immediately, but you *will* see it when you change your mindset. I'm here to help you. I might not have a Ph.D. – I graduated from the University of Life. But what a life! I'm so grateful for each and every experience that has led me to this happy spot. It hasn't been easy, but that's why I'm going to help you listen to your Monk!

I'm going to share with you some steps which have changed my life and hopefully will change yours too, but I just want to mention a few things first. Unlike other books that will promise you this and promise you that, I can't promise that my techniques will work for you. There's a good chance they will. A very good chance! But even though we are both human beings, we're different. Different things work for different people at different times.

What took me a day or month, or a year may take you less, or you might need to tweak each idea to make it work for you. Some things I love to do might not appeal to you. But before you dismiss it without trying, give it a go with an open mind, and if it doesn't work think of ways you can adapt it. For example, maybe you work night shifts and can't go to sleep at the time I suggest, then you can come up with your own schedule that works for you.

If you adapt my tips to fit in with your life, over time, they will 100% work. I'm proof of that!

It took me a few years to get to this level of fulfillment. So, if you are looking for a quick fix, you won't find it here. Sorry! (Not sorry.) This is a healing process which takes time, and, although you may not like to hear this, most of the time you probably will be better off going through it alone. Yeah, you heard me! ALONE! If you're afraid to be alone then you'll never face your other fears or tackle the Monkey thoughts inside of you.

It's often only when we are alone that we can truly face these obstacles. It's like being a kid in your room calling out to your mom and dad because there are monsters in the closet. Your parents come into your room and tell you there is no such thing. They leave the room, and you're on your own to face your fears. Eventually you realize your mom and dad were right. There aren't any monsters under the bed. The feeling you get from conquering your fear is incredible. Would you get to that point if your parents never left you alone?

But as a child, it took you time to learn that the worst monsters are all in your head, and you don't have to fear your closet. At first, your mom and dad might have left a small light on in your room, maybe sung you a song to settle you down for the night. Gradually, you learned how to go to sleep without a small light or a song because you focused on the light inside of you and calmed yourself. That's how you learned you could do it.

That's just how we are going to face your fears, but although you have to do the work yourself, you're not totally on your own. You've got me to guide you every step of the way. Together, we're going to focus on the light inside of you - your Monk.

What I'm about to share with you is my way of looking at *energy*. Some call it God, the Universe, Buddha, or even Jesus. For the purposes of this book, I'm going to call that divine concept "energy." Bear with me. It will all make sense as we go on.

After several experiences in my life, the ups and the downs, I started to question what this energy was doing, this energy I believed in unquestioningly. I'm not saying I stopped believing in it, but I wanted some answers.

Remember the story of Adam and Eve in the Bible? Was it really about a snake seducing them to eat the apple? Or was it the thoughts in their minds which played the biggest role in their decision?

With all due respect to the Bible, it's a very old text whose author is unknown. We weren't alive at the time it was written nor have any idea what was really going on then, apart from what the Bible claims happened.

After Adam and Eve's story, the "system" (school) usually jumps to the Cain and Abel story. The Bible says they were the first two sons of Adam and Eve, a fact which Wikipedia agrees with, so it must be true, right?

Now, if you're not familiar with the story of Cain and Abel, Cain, the firstborn, was a farmer, and his younger brother Abel was a shepherd. The brothers made sacrifices to God, each of his own produce, but God favored Abel's sacrifices over Cain's. Unsurprisingly, Cain was not impressed, although that doesn't excuse what happened next. He murdered Abel, whereupon Yahweh punished Cain by condemning him to a life of wandering. Cain subsequently dwelt in the land of "Nod" (נוֹד – "wande" and "ring"), where he built a city and fathered multiple children starting with Enoch.

Why am I telling you all this? Well, if Cain and Abel were Adam and Eve's firstborn children, and no one was there with them, how was Cain able to build a city? How could he have children? And what is the point of putting a mark on his head if there were only three people left in the world? What the Bible forgot to include is that Adam and Eve had more children.

But I digress. As I said, I had a lot of questions. But my questions weren't about the stories. They were more about wondering what had led these people to make the choices they did.

- Was it God's hand?
- Was it this energy that surrounds us?
- Was it our minds?
- How do our minds work?
- What are those voices in our heads?
- Can we control those voices?
- What is this so-called conscience that keeps defining what is right and what is wrong?
- Are there really Monks or Monkeys?

I gave these questions much thought. I read, I put into practice what I read, and I pondered more, and I lived, which is the best way to learn. I decided I wanted to figure out my own point of view about the nature of God, Monks, and the Monkey. Who is pulling the strings here?

Some of you may agree with me, and some of you may not and that is fine. Please, take some time and see what works for you. For me, if I find things that work, things that make sense, I want to share them. Well, if I'm honest, I'm bursting to share them! That's what inspired me to write my first book *F*ck Your Past*, where I discussed my life struggles and how I overcame them. I mentioned my fears, particularly my fear of losing whatever I thought was good for me, whether that be my job, my friends, my girlfriend, etc.

I realized, over time of course, that the incorrect choices I made came from one place. Fear. **FEAR!** *The fear of losing the things and people I loved!*

It may be the same for you, fear is often behind a lot of problems. As soon as I realized the cause of my fears, it was so much easier to contain them. However, I wanted to understand more about this feeling, this feeling of fear, and why it is that we so easily allow it to rule us.

- Why is it so easy to feed our fear (Monkey) than feeding our happiness? (Monk)
- Why is fear more contagious than happiness?

Yes, I had so many thoughts and questions. Did I find the answers? Read on, then let me know if you think I have!

Chapter One: Are You Listening to Your Monkey Mind?

For years, I was scratching my head wondering why I continued to have the same issues over and over. I'd start something, a job, a business or a relationship. Everything was great in the beginning, so great that I'd quickly get a better position at work, earn more money, while my relationships were almost too good to be true. Yep, I was on a happy roll, baby!

And then one day, slowly, it all started to fall apart. Why, WHY?

I look back and I can see just how much impact I had on what happened. Bad moves, bad decisions, me listening to the Monkey, and fear kicking in, all of which led to stress, which led to less sleep, which led to mistakes, which led to feeling down and negative and anxious, which led to *losing it all!!*

Every single time something went disastrously wrong, the same question slapped me in the face: *How the f.ck did I get to this point?!* Then the finger-pointing began. Who can I blame for it this time? (Apart from myself, of course!) Well, let me make myself clear.

Although you might like to blame our parents, your partner, your colleagues, that annoying person on the internet, for how you behave in life, it really is on you and only you. This might sound depressing, but it's liberating because it means you have the power to change things!

I'm going to explain this a bit more by sharing a little about my life and how it affected my decisions over the years until I found the source of my issues: the fear of losing something. Losing a girl, I was seeing, or losing my job.

If I'm honest, I wasn't afraid of not having work. It's easy to get a job, but I discovered that it was the environment of the workplace, the camaraderie, the hang-out times, the community feeling that I didn't want to lose. Unfortunately, this led me to stay at jobs when I knew I should leave. I had several fears about work:

- What will people think of me if I leave?
- How would it look on my resume?
- If I make this move, will it be the right move?

- What if I lose the friends I've made here?

The problem with these fears is that they were blocks I was putting up between myself and my goals. It's great to have lists and steps you need to take to reach your goals and we'll get into that more soon. But there's no point to these lists if there's something blocking you from progressing. And what is that big block many of us face which causes you to waste time and not achieve your goals? Say it with me! FEAR.

That fearful voice we can call the Monkey is always inside us, trying to sway us to the dark side. Others call it the monkey mind, that cheeky monkey trying to drag you into his mischief! While I like the image of a naughty monkey always trying to get between me and my dream life, in this book, I'm using the concept of the Monkey, just because I think it sounds a little more serious than a cute little monkey. And believe me, this fear/ Monkey is serious!

It's true people tend to listen to the negative thoughts of the Monkey more than any of the positive ones that the Monk tries to shine through, especially during difficult times in their lives. You know it's true!

Think about when you're having a bad day, and someone cuts you off in traffic or says something offensive to you. Do you take a breath, are you grateful for this moment no matter how irritating, and thank God for the opportunity to learn patience and tolerance? Maybe you are that evolved and if so, you don't need to read on!

But I'm guessing you're more likely to curse, say something equally offensive, and blame someone else for this issue/ situation/day you are having.

You're going along with the Monkey's thoughts that first pop into your head. Why? It may well date back to a more primitive time when we had to be on constant alert for danger. We have a drive to overthink situations to keep us safe from harm. Fair enough. But now, when our world is generally safe and we don't need to worry about tigers ambushing us while out hunting, we need to keep this Monkey in line. He's just causing trouble.

Yes, we do need to question situations. We are human with human emotions and sometimes we have trouble controlling them. That's fine. Even with all the hard work I've done listening to my Monk,

I still snap if something bothers me, especially if I'm going through a rough time. But these days, I can better recognize and understand where that anger and frustration is coming from. And you will too. Like anything, it's all practice. So, when the Monkey makes an appearance, I now can stop myself from believing him or giving in to those thoughts and decide to listen to my Monk and choose love over that fearful thought.

Your Monk is there to rescue you from the Monkey. We can't let our Monk help us if we are not even aware of the Monkey's thoughts.

I want to try a fun little exercise with you to see what kind of mindset you have and how much you let the Monkey rule your mind. Let's see if you can recognize your Monkey's thoughts or Monk's thoughts, and which of the two has more power at this time. Go, Monks! Boo, Monkeys!

Before you read on, I want you to go about your day as normal but pay attention to your thoughts throughout the day. Try to be an objective witness of your behavior, how you treat people, how you treat yourself, how you act when issues arise. Do you explode? Do you automatically assume the worst? Do you complain and blame others? Or do you take control of the situation with ease?

See if you have more:

- Happy thoughts.
- Judgmental thoughts.
- Thoughts of love, or hate, resentment, or longing.

Ask yourself:

- Are you smiling in your mind, or crying?
- Do you have consistent thoughts about work stress?
- Are you cursing people in your head?
- Do you want to hug everyone you see?
- Do you feel powerful or weak when you wake up?
- Do you point fingers at others, or do you accept responsibility for putting yourself in any given situation?

I could go on and on, but you probably get the picture by now. By the end of the day, you should have a clearer picture of the kind of person you are, which may surprise you. We are often not *aware* of the fears blocking us from seeing things clearly. We let fear/the Monkey take residence in our minds and lead us to do the wrong actions, conclusions, or decisions in life. And then, unfortunately, we suffer the consequences.

I don't think I need to point out that fear isn't always bad. Sometimes we do need to listen to our fears, but I think we know the difference between a truly fearful situation and a situation which is fearful due to negative thoughts. Fear can help us escape real danger but can also paralyze us into inaction. We must always check in with ourselves to ask:

- Is this fear helpful or unhelpful right now?

- Is it stopping me from moving forward towards what I want/need/dream about?
- Is it saving me from real danger?

I'm serious here. I really want you to take time out before reading on to pay attention to what's truly going on in your mind. Take note of your thoughts. Remember, the point of this game is to try to figure out which part of your mind you listen to more: the Monkey's or Monk's. Don't be discouraged if you find the Monkey is winning by a mile. Now that you're aware, you're already halfway to winning the battle.

Check on that Monkey:
- Is he pushing more and more fear into your life?

- Is he showing you only one side of the story?
- Is he saying that nothing else matters except his words?
- Does he ever let the Monk speak? If so, when?

Check on your Monk:
- Can you hear him? Or is the Monkey too loud?
- If you do hear him, do you believe what he is saying?

Remember, the Monkey might make promises, telling you that he's the only one who can keep you safe or give you what you wish. But really, if you follow his advice, there will be a cost. The cost of losing your mind or those you love. The cost of losing out on leveling up your life. It's like a movie script by Walt Disney himself, right? But remember, all Disney movies have a happy ending, and your life can too!

The Monkey comes bearing an apple - you know the story. But no one is in your head but you. You don't have to eat the apple! You have to ignore the Monkey, no matter how tempting his words are. You can't blame others for what's going through your head and how you got there. I've said it before, and I'll say it again - it's all on **you**!

But you can still change today and tomorrow if you decide to choose love and happiness, if we decide to listen to your Monk more than your Monkey. And guess what? The more you listen to your Monk, the louder his voice becomes. He will get stronger and stronger. How great is that?

Chapter Two: Stop Saying
I Should Do, Instead
Let's Start Doing!

We spend a great deal of time talking about what we "should" do. You know what you "should" do at work to be more productive, to get a raise. But we can use the same methods in order to change or adjust things in ourselves, give our lives a raise! The good thing here too is that when you improve your personal life, it naturally flows into your work life. It's a win-win!

As I said, and I'm being repetitive for a reason, being aware and recognizing the Monkey's thoughts is a massive step towards stopping them. If you can go a step further and note down those Monkey's thoughts/feelings or mindset whenever you notice them, you will progress much faster and see genuine long-term change.

But start small. There is no rush. You can't skip over the first steps, and it's worth building the right foundation before you move forward. Each step must be made carefully in order to make bigger progress.

So, when you note down the Monkey's thoughts, you get closer to the heart of the fear which is haunting you. You begin to understand where this fear is coming from and face it. Most likely this fear is from your past, and not just the near past. You will probably find it stems from your childhood. Many situations occur when we are young which we don't think affected us because we didn't quite understand what was going on. Don't discount the power of the past. Events which occurred early on in your life, some of them seemingly trivial, are the likely cause of most if not all your fears now.

I can't tell you what yours are. That's for you to find out, which is why I advise you to do the mindset exercise. I *can* tell you that mine were from my mom and one of the biggest was the fear of my dad leaving and not coming back. Consequently, I had a fear of letting go and moving on. Those fears were very real to me until I hit thirty-eight years of age. Seriously.

The only time I had any relief from these fears was when I had to go into the army, which turned out to be a place of structure for me. I didn't need to worry about what would or could happen next. What a relief that was! All I needed to do was to serve my country, which basically included:

- Waking up early
- Practice tactics
- Patrols
- Missions
- Eating
- Sleeping early
- Going home to visit family
- Having fun

I did this over and over for three years and got paid for it. (A small amount but it was enough for me at the time.)

I was eighteen years old when I joined the army, and twenty-one years old when I left. I certainly wasn't prepared for what came next — life! Maybe you felt the same when you left school or college. When you are out in the world without those structures, support, and social networks, it can be daunting. At the time, I thought I was fearless! No one could touch me.

But as I grew older, I became more and more emotional. I was always fighting a battle with myself, trying to figure out what I wanted from life.

I was lucky. I was given plenty of opportunities, so lack of options wasn't my problem. My problem was the opposite — I didn't make the right choices when I had the chance to. I'd let ego and fear interfere with my life. Oh, that Monkey!

I let people's opinions affect me and took it all personally. I let the Monkey say whatever it wanted and soaked it all up. At the time, I didn't understand that the only reason people said mean things to me was because they feared or were envious of me. They feared what I could do when or if I understood the power I possessed. They feared I would start believing in myself and do what they were doing but better. The Monkey-Devil really was wearing Prada while he was strutting inside my head day and night. So much so that I started to believe that my dreams were too big for me.

It was a kind of personal hell alright. I didn't know where I was going with my life, I didn't have any passion left, so I just dragged along like a zombie with no direction at all. Not a good feeling. I lost interest in love and being loved. Little did I know, that was the key right there. Love! There's just got to be love, love, love.

Chapter Three: A Balance Life Is a Happy Life

Before I go any further, I want to touch on friendships. I really hope during this book I can open your mind to a concept of friendship that will really benefit your life. What friendship means to you now may not be the same after you read this book. Beware! I want to share how I see friendship now. To start, I want you to think carefully about the people in your life:

- Why are they still around you?
- Why are you still around them?
- If you don't feel you want them in your life, why do you fear letting them go?

- Why are you still friends with this person/ group of people who you know will not be there for you the way you are for them?
- Why can't you just say, "Bye, bitch. I'm out!"?
- Why are you so afraid to move on from this person?
- Why are you so afraid to be by yourself?
- What is stopping you from finding new friends?

The answer to why we keep toxic people around is simple: Fear.

BALANCE

You might wonder "why do I have to suffer the consequences of bad decisions?" Why can't everyone just be good and do the right thing that serves us all best? Well, if God or that energy which brought us to life wanted us to be good all the time or wanted our world to be a purely happy place, then he wouldn't have put temptation before Adam and Eve's eyes. They'd still be living in the Garden of Eden, no matter how many apples they ate.

Our world is set up to be balanced. That's how it is, whether we like it or not. Unfortunately, this balance is not fair most of the time. You only have to look at the news to see stories about cold and hungry homeless people, or the countless people who live in horrible circumstances.

I must note here I don't and can't know any of the circumstances of these people's stories, how they feel, or how they came to be in this miserable situation. But I believe that if we can, we must help them out to where they want to be.

However, I'm going to caveat that with a controversial thought. Would you believe me if I told you that some people who are suffering (note, *some* of them) wanted to live this way? Sounds weird right? But it is true. Let me explain.

Last summer I was going about my regular Friday routine where I buy food from the market next door and give it to the homeless people around my area. (One of the most fulfilling aspects of getting my life on track is that I'm in a place where I am now able to help others!)

At first, these people were surprised to see someone doing this, someone out of the blue arriving with bags of hot chicken during Covid times. I did it all summer, every Friday, and gradually they became friendlier, trusted me, and began to wait for me to come, knowing they could count on me.

As the year slowly progressed into a cold NYC winter, the government, due to Covid, placed all the homeless people into hotels. Each Friday I noticed the homeless people near my area were decreasing, except for a few who stayed on the street. They stayed not because they didn't have the option to go to a hotel, but because they liked where they were. How could this be? Wouldn't anyone prefer a warm and safe hotel room to sleeping on the hard freezing streets?

This question led me to a TV show idea which I subsequently pitched to a known producer who told me, "I've looked into this strange phenomenon before, too. Some of those who we approached to help settle them into a hotel just did not want to be helped. They enjoyed their life as it was. We simply can't force them to do something they don't want to do. And as long as they are not doing anything illegal, the city won't intervene, and basically gives up on them."

I'm telling you this because the balance in the world is in fact equal, and the only reason we think it is not due to the media/news. The universe has got its act together even if we can't see it.

Can we try to make things better? Yes! Should we try to make things better? Yes!

Even if we give it one hundred percent of our attention, we will need everyone, and I mean *everyone's* support to change it. This delicate balance between the bad and the good is important. That is why we have the Cain and Abel story - the bad boy kills the good, and in a way, gets away with it. If we wanted a fair story, Cain should have died too.

According to the story, God decided to put a mark on his head, so that no one would hurt him but didn't take away any of his abilities to build a new city, which he did.

Finding Your Balance

Balance is the key to life. If we have a balanced mind, we make good decisions. To be balanced we need self-awareness. If we make bad decisions with a balanced mind, we can learn from these mistakes; we can control our emotions and deal with the results of the bad decision. Basically, we get on with it! With a balanced mind, we are also able to detach ourselves from those who don't want the best for us and build connections with those who do. Super important!

But how do we get to this balanced mindset? What is stopping us from having it?

I'm reading an amazing book called *The One Thing*. In one chapter (chapter eight to be exact), the author talks about "a balanced life." He discusses the idea that a balanced life is a lie — the idea of balance is exactly that: an idea. In philosophy, "The Golden Mean" is the moderate middle between two positions where one state is more desirable than another state. In other words, he says that we always want more balance, but don't know how to "measure" balance.

I both agree and disagree with him. Yes, balance is a philosophical idea, but at the same time, we don't know what balance means because no one ever explained to us the idea of a balanced life — unless you count looking at someone else's grass thinking it's greener. We've all been there!

As a kid, do you remember going to one of your friend's houses to play, and having a moment when you wished your parents were the same as your friend's parents? That they acted the same, were as fun, or less strict, or stricter and less fun? Or that you had what they had? You pictured them having the perfect life when really you had no idea of what's going on behind closed doors. You don't see them fight, you think they never fight, that they don't have issues, that they have a blissful life with no worries.

This is an example of a fake balance. I mean let's face it, we are all on our best behavior when we have guests over. We're not going to argue with the kids over their homework or bicker with our partners in front of witnesses if we can avoid it.

This is a sort of a "balance lie." You're not getting the full picture, so you can't know how good or bad someone's life really is. But to say it's *all* a lie is like saying every person in the world is evil, that everyone is fake, and no one is what they seem. That's not true either. I hear rumors that some families never fight. I don't know of any of them, but I'm sure there are some, somewhere?! What I do know though, is life isn't like the Brady Bunch *all* the time!

To measure balance in your life isn't easy, and what that looks like is going to be different for each one of us. In order to have a healthy balance in your life that suits you, you need to change your reality. At least, if you're not happy at this point in your life. If you *are* perfectly happy, have life all balanced out, well, what are you doing reading this book? Go and write your own! I know I'd love to read it.

So back to us strugglers trying to achieve a healthy balance in our lives. How do you do that? You know things are not right, but you're either ignoring it, hoping things will just fix themselves, or unaware of what's really going on.

A healthy balance is a healthy life, and a healthy life is a happy life.

Being happy doesn't necessarily mean that we need to travel somewhere new and exciting every week or go out partying with different people every night. You can be happy doing the same thing every day if you love what you do!

For example, if you love your work, then you have fun while doing it. That's the ideal, isn't it? You don't need external validation in order to have fun. The funny part about finding your balance is that you don't need to look far away at all because the real key to happiness is being you and loving yourself. It's turning your back on what you 'should' do, or what the media says will make you happy. Remember, they're in the business of making money by selling you stuff you don't need! They're telling you that you'll find happiness if you only buy yourself new clothes, a new home, a new car, get thinner and fitter, have a little facelift or go on an expensive holiday. Don't buy into the lies!

Loving yourself goes deeper than loving how you look in front of the mirror. We all know that. But do we *really* know it? Deep inside? You've just got to look inside yourself and love who you are, buddy! Love. Who. You. Are.

Are you even aware of how you talk to yourself about yourself? Are you hearing your Monk? Or is the Monkey running the show? Each of us requires a different balance which is why we live different lives. We are all dealing with our own issues. So, what may be a happy and balanced life for me may be boring for you.

I have a friend who's not happy unless she's socializing, exercising, or out and about all the frigging time. To me, that's *way* too busy. There's no balance there for me! But for her, being home reading philosophical books about life, with a dog curled up by her side does not cut it for her. She'd be so bored.

Know and be aware of who you are, what you want, what you enjoy, and what **you** need to feel balanced. We need to figure out within ourselves what makes us feel balanced according to *our* lives.

This is serious! Listen up! Because others often can't help themselves. They have to try to get you to live in a way that *they* feel is balanced for you and can influence you. Comments such as, "Gee, you need to get out more," or "You've become boring," or, "You're too busy, you need to relax," etc. can take a toll and you can find yourself going along with what others want, which leads to an imbalance.

Don't let people guilt you into living your life according to their needs and preferences. I have another friend who adores being home. She'd spend a lot of time out at clubs when she was younger and is happy with her quiet life now. My super social friend was worried about her, thinking she wasn't getting out enough and tried to persuade her to get out more, but why would she want to do that? She loves being home, reading, pottering, recharging from her busy job!

People need to respect how each of us chooses to live our lives – just as you need to respect them. Are you living their life or your life? Is societal pressure making you feel something *is* wrong with your life? If so, maybe you need to move on from some friendships, or away from people who just don't accept you, or who don't get where you are headed. Take another look over my questions regarding friendships, get your ass in gear, and do what you need to do!

Have you ever seen the movie *The Lion King*? If you have, do you remember the beginning of the story when Simba and his dad Mufasa go for the first-morning patrol, and Mufasa talks about the circle of life. Mufasa explains to his young son that, "a king's time as ruler rises and falls like the sun. One day, Simba, the sun will set on my time here, and will rise with you as the new king." He goes on to tell him that as the next king, Simba's duty is to look for what he can give and protect his kingdom. There is a balance to this world, every creature has its purpose, from the tiniest ant to the most graceful antelope. As Mufasa puts it, "When we die, our bodies become the grass, and the antelope eats the grass. Everything is connected in the great circle of life."

As I mentioned before, balance is a way of understanding our existence and respecting those around us, the good and the bad. We are all bad in our own way, and good in our own way. What matters is the amount of good that we do in order to find the balance in between.

The kind of balance I'm talking about isn't measured as 50/50. I don't mean that you should live a life which has equal amounts of highs and lows. No, this balance is measured by the happiness you feel within yourself; your feelings of fulfillment, and whether you're happy with where you're at in your life. It is also measured by the good you do for others.

But think about it. When you do good, do you have expectations? If you do, you're asking for disappointment if you do it with an attitude that people owe you something or need to help you the way you helped them. That's not how life works. If you want to give, you must give without the expectation of something in return. That is where real fulfillment and happiness live.

I'll give you an example. There was once a kid my buddies and I used to make fun of all the time. I'm not proud to admit that when I was a young boy I used to hang out with the wrong people, people who had their own way of doing business and handling people. It happens.

In my religion, there is a festival where we pray to God for our sins and ask for his forgiveness. This holiday is called "Yom Kippur," and during this time we don't eat for twenty-four hours. Before this holiday, there is a period when we read a specific prayer, called "Forgiveness Days." As a kid, we used to joke about the types of people who did so much good all year round, yet before Yom Kippur and until the end of the holiday you can find all of them singing asking God for forgiveness. As fun or stupid as it sounds, that was their idea of balance.

I'm going to show you how I found my balance, hoping it will help you to find yours.

As I mentioned in my first book, happiness is a choice. You can wake up in the morning deciding you want to be happy today, no matter what happens, and listen to your Monk. Or you can decide you don't want to be happy and listen to the Monkey's negativity all day long. No one is there to force you either way!

It all starts with how you manage your bedtime and morning routine. Some things to consider:

- What time do you go to sleep at night?
- What time do you wake up?
- How do you wake up?
- Do you have the right bed for you?
- Do you have the right pillow for you?
- Do you have the right person next to you? (Or pet!)
- All the above needs to be comfortable and consistent for us to rest well and be happy. I myself made the following changes to my life with wonderful results:
- I changed my sleeping habits.
- I began sleep meditation.

- I repeated a few positive words before bed and when after waking up.
- I meditated/prayed immediately after waking up.
- I listened to relaxing sounds.
- I hit the gym with some cheery wake-up sounds that make me want to sing and dance!
- I take a regular shower with a splash of cold water before I get out. Note: Taking a shower doesn't just clean your physical body, it also cleans your aura. When you get out of the shower after a good scrub, pay attention to the relief you feel. Embrace that feeling. It's a similar sensation to a cool breeze on a hot day. If you want to take anything to a higher level, really, the first thing you need to do is purify or cleanse

yourself. Make space for whatever you want to invite in. This applies to anything in life. Without purifying your body and your mind, you will not be able to manifest or achieve anything.

- I keep my home tidy and clean, for the same reasons as above.
- I changed a few words in my thought patterns to more positive ones.

Let me explain where I wanted to see myself when I felt that things were not going as planned. I knew the opportunities I wanted in my life were there, but I just stuck to the same negative circle, which led me to having the same results in a downward spiral.

For me, a balanced life was being able to pay my bills and have a girlfriend who supported me (and vice versa) on every level, no matter what. That sounded simple and easy to achieve, right? At least in my head, it was.

I made sure I had a job that paid enough to cover my bills, and I was sure I had the right attitude to maintain a stable relationship, regardless of the girl I was dating. But I wanted to do more, so I put my hand up for more hours. My work ethic was strong, and I thought that if I worked hard, both at work and in my romantic relationships, I would eventually be noticed, respected, and rewarded by my boss, partner, and everyone. But instead, it was stressful as f.ck! The amount of effort and work I was pouring into my job didn't pay off. My relationships were far from the balanced vision I had in my head, and it was not a good feeling!

So, what was I doing wrong? Well, the idea started to become clear when I realized just how easy it was for me to get what I wanted by doing less work.

That's right. I could achieve a better balance and enjoy more abundance with less work. Sounds good, right? Too good to be true? Now, when I say less work, I don't mean I was sitting down and waiting for things to come to me. Of course, you won't get anywhere like that, not even with the law of attraction! (And here's a little-known secret many books don't tell you. With the law of attraction, it's not just about visualizing what you want – you have to actually work towards it too!)

What I mean by doing less, is focusing on your "should do" list and not wasting precious time and effort on the "can do" list. Why? Because if you focus on the things you can do, you don't really improve your set of skills. You just go on repeating something that you already know, repeatedly. There's no leveling up this way, guys!

But when you focus on things you should do it means you want to discover what you don't know, but which will be helpful to you in the future. For example, let's say you're a basketball player and you already know how to dribble and get into the paint without being blocked. What you suck at, though, is shooting from the free-throw line and the three-point line.

If you *avoid* the should-dos here, which is practicing your free-throw and three-point shots, you'll be easy to guard whenever you try to make those shots. But if you focus on your should-do — three-point shooting — you'll be harder to guard, your defender will need to stay closer in case you decide to shoot, which will make life much easier if you decide to dribble to the paint.

If you're not into basketball and you haven't got a clue what I'm going on about with paint and dribble, think of it like this: If you keep doing something you already know how to do and avoid doing things that will improve your life, then you will never see progress in your life. Keep doing what you're doing, and you'll keep seeing the same results. It's as simple as that.

Make a to-do list every morning and mark each item on the list as a can-do or a should-do. Moving forward, keep your focus on the should-dos, when making your list. Keep it short and simple to set yourself up for success. Don't put unnecessary extra pressure on yourself.

Just one small step towards your goals every day will see you make huge progress by the end of the year.

I mean sure it's possible to finish a long to-do list, but have you done everything on that list well? You can rush through each one, and do a crappy job but say **yes,** I finished my list. But this approach can leave you feeling like you didn't do SHIIIIIIIIIIIIIIT!

The whole point of a good list is to focus on a small number of just three things you should do that you know will improve your life significantly. Give them your 100% attention to get the most benefit from those things. Once you've mastered every should do, make a new list. And **that** is the meaning behind "doing less."

Chapter Four: If You Change Your Habits, You Will Change Your Life

Changing your habits is one of the most important steps you can take towards a better, healthier life. When I was younger, going out partying was fun, but it was also exhausting. I mean I had fun for almost thirty years! At some point in your life, you start to ask yourself "WTF am I doing here?"

If you've been putting partying as your highest priority, eventually, you're going to get sick of it. I'm not saying you need to stop having any fun if you want to improve your life. I'm saying that there are other ways to enjoy yourself! Other new ways you'll find even more fulfilling.

As people we grow, we change, and hopefully, we evolve, develop new interests. But in order to truly evolve, you need to be aware of what you're doing, and why. Quite often the reason you need this type of escapist fun is due to wanting to escape your unhappy life. When you really think about it, isn't it true?

Today what I call a happy life, may seem boring to you, but what if I tell you, it's only boring because of your perspective? For example, in my job, something's always going wrong. It's very rare that in the construction industry things go smoothly. Even though most of the issues which keep coming up are pretty much the same all the time, it's still challenging and exciting for me.

There are always subtle differences and for that reason, I don't get bored.

My other daily routine involves learning about industries or subjects in which I want to do better in. Again, this might sound boring to you, but to me, it lights up my brain and life. It's fun!

I love riding my city bike. It makes me feel young. I love walking with my dog or by myself. Having dinner and going to the gym makes me happy! All of these make up my healthy day-to-day routine which I love. And if you have the right girl or boyfriend by your side, you really don't need anything else.

I'm loving my life right now. Less drama, fewer headaches, less ego. Less time wasted on meaningless crap. More love, and more love, and adding a bit more love will make your life easier and happier. Yeah, baby!

Sure, I still have bad days. Life isn't perfect. There are still those ups and downs. Just like anyone, most of the time, I improve, go back a little, then go forwards again. The main thing is that, overall, I'm moving forward. I'm about to share with you next will take time, so go easy on yourself when you start doing it. You might see/feel a difference in a month, or perhaps three months. It may even take a full year. It's all good.

The goal behind all these suggestions is for you to be able to recognize the Monkey and his *Monkeyish* ways more clearly. It's all about awareness. Once you achieve more awareness of the Monkey, the more easily you can make changes. I mean how can you fix a problem if you don't know it's there? Are you aware the tap is leaking? Nope? Then there's no way you're going to be able to fix it. Can you hear the drip, drip of the tap? Aha. *Now* you can fix it!

And why do you want to more clearly recognize the Monkey inside of you? Because he's holding you back from achieving your potential. Once you are aware of the Monkey and his Monkeyishness, every time he talks to you, you'll be able to take a moment and reflect on that fear This will allow you to become present and connect to your Monk instead of the Monkey. This will center your body, your mind, your soul, your heart. You want to get to a point where you master this cycle. Then, your old habits will easily shift to new and healthy ones, creating the perfect balance in your life.

Chapter Five: Making Things Easy for Ourselves

Did you ever stop for a second and ask yourself why you have negative thoughts? Do you ever wonder why you overthink, causing you to doubt life, and yourself?

I know it might sound stupid, but for a long, long, long time, I didn't think I was an attractive guy. Now, I know everyone is attractive in their own way! This self-doubt was so stupid that it ended up becoming my reality.

It was just so silly because the girls I was dating were always the most beautiful, at least on the outside. I had proof literally in my arms that I was attractive, so why did I still hold onto this fear, this Monkey feeling that having the girlfriend I'd dreamed of was just an illusion? That one day they would leave me because I wasn't good-looking enough, or a good enough person for them. What I didn't understand was that my fear of losing them was what pushed them away. Yep, my fears became my reality. (And yes, in the same way, your dreams can become your reality too! Exciting huh? But more of that later.)

So why did it take me so long to understand this seemingly basic concept? Why did I hold onto my fear so strongly instead of questioning it? And what helped me change my mind?

As soon as I found an awesome girl who was interested in me, I was all for it. However, as soon as we got together, I started questioning, is this for real? How did I end up with this girl? Does she really like me the same way? Man, am I dreaming?

Those questions (that Monkey!) spinning around my head led me to trying too hard and messing up so many situations. Since I felt like my girlfriend was about to leave me, I clung on, and instead pushed her away. No one likes clingy!

Have you started dating someone who talked about their ex all the time so you feel like this ex will come back into their life in some way? Have you had one of those moments where your ego kicks in, your fear comes knocking on your shoulder and says, "Yo! Can you see what's going to happen? She's going to leave you for her ex! What are you going to do about it?!"

The Monkey is at it again! As soon as you start listening to that Monkey, you are in stress mode! You start thinking about how you can stop her from leaving you. How can you win her over, so she stays with you and does not leave you for him?

This whole idea of winning something back that you already have is stupid, isn't it? In hindsight, I can look back and see how illogical I was being, but at the time, I couldn't see it.

So, when you have this crazy idea of winning something you already have, you've already lost.

Remember, the Monkey's voice is stronger than the Monk's, but that doesn't mean the Monkey is stronger. No, it's more that he is louder, more persistent and appeals to that human nature which finds it easier to see the negatives over the positives.

Going back to the Adam and Eve story where they were thrown out of paradise because they ate the apple, they were a lesson to us all. Unfortunately, though, instead of learning that lesson, we keep getting attracted to the negatives more than the positives, so it's hard for us to see the good when it's right there in front of us.

I missed out on lots of great relationships because my fear had a grip on me. Even if I didn't like how I looked in the mirror, it seemed that whomever I was able to attract, saw something different. Instead of seeing that as a positive, as something which proved I was wrong, I chose to think it was a dream. A dream or fantasy that I needed to fight to keep hold of instead of embracing it and enjoying the moment. It's really hard to see what is in front of you if you are not happy with your life and with yourself. It takes a lot of work to get there, but it all starts with YOU! If you truly want to be aware of your habits and want to make the effort to change them, and truly want a better life for yourself, you can.

As I said, I'm still human and have my bad days. Just because I've changed my habits doesn't mean life doesn't slap me here and there. The difference is that now, for every slap, I thank God or the universe for the lesson. I learn, I let go, and most importantly, I forgive the situation and myself. I forgive myself for getting in that position and forgive those who let me down.

Let's choose love over those thoughts, (the Monkey's thoughts,) and *move the f.ck on!!* In order to be able to get to this mindset, you need to ask the right question. When I say the right question, I mean the *one* question that will make everything else easier.

If you have an issue in a relationship, ask yourself: What is the *one* thing I can do today so that it will not happen again? This question applies to any other situation you struggle with. By focusing on *one* thing, it will ease the process of getting where you want to be. Because it all can be overwhelming sometimes, figuring out how do I change? Where do I start?

Focusing on *one* thing may seem like you're slowing the process of manifesting the life you want. But slow is good. Small steps are good for a bigger change. Slow and steady wins the race!

I want you to start asking yourself every morning when you wake up and every night before you go to bed, this *one* question. **What is the one thing I can do today (or tomorrow if it is evening) to make everything easier?**

When you include this question as part of your daily routine, you will be fully engaged in getting the results you are looking for. You're *aware* of what you want, and what you need to do. If you need some help figuring out your one thing, here's some of the most powerful things I've done which have changed my life:

1. **Change your sleep habits**

I usually like to wake up between 6and 7a.m. The days, I usually wake at 6 a.m., I usually don't need an alarm to wake me up. When I was depressed, waking up was *hard*! But as soon as I started to feel good about myself and where I was going in life, waking up at 6 a.m. became normal and easy. One day I was using YouTube for my meditation video, and an advertisement came up, discussing the brain, and when it is at its most effective. It stated that the best time to go to sleep is around 10 p.m. with a wake up of around 4 a.m. Four a.m.?! Yikes! But I was curious, so I kept watching and they said that all the billionaires do this. That's when my ears really perked up! Who doesn't want to be a billionaire? So, I investigated this further, and found this sleep and wake up routine: Protects the heart.

- Reduces the risk of cancer.
- Boosts energy.
- Improves the immune system.
- Improves skin conditions.

- Controls body weight.
- Improves confidence.
- Enhances organization skills. (Your early morning hours tend to be the most productive time of day because you get uninterrupted time to yourself.)
- Reduces stress.
- Makes you feel happier.
- Gives you added time to exercise.
- Increases brain activity and focus.
- Improves your sleep cycles.
- Greatly enhances your daily productivity.
- Promotes overall positive mental health and well-being.

Sounds good?! Now, these results have all been scientifically studied, so you don't just have to take my word for it. At first, I thought it would be hard to wake up around that time and be fully focused and motivated, but surprisingly it wasn't as bad as I thought. I was already getting up at 6 a.m., but I usually found myself waking up anyway around 4 a.m. for some unknown reason. All I needed to do was just push myself out of bed when that happened, so I did and the results of doing this were amazing!

I gained a wonderful appreciation of the silence in the morning, the peace, the sound of the birds, the differences between each bird sound, the morning wind, the sunrises, the morning skyline... I could go on and on about how amazing it is. But most importantly as soon as you try this, you will find more balance in your routine. You will see how much time you have on your hands to do whatever you want and accomplish more. What a great feeling! Instead of franticly rushing, my mornings are slow and full of purpose. It's extraordinary how much I can fit into my morning now.

I can include:

- Morning meditation.
- Prayer.
- A workout at the gym.
- Walking my dog.
- Hot water with lemon, then my black coffee.
- Reading a book and writing this one!
- Dealing with emails.
- Watching sports news.
- Getting ready to start my workday.

All of this in a three-hour window between 4 to 7 a.m.! Shifting when you wake up isn't just about what you can accomplish. It's that amazing feeling of embracing a beautiful morning, before going on to be the first person in the office with a smile on your face. The boss will love you! Wouldn't you rather arrive fresh-faced and relaxed rather than carrying that frazzled look — you know, the one that tells everyone you woke up just fifteen minutes earlier, raced out the door without breakfast, your heart beating rapidly with stress, and clutching a coffee? The thing is, that stressed, rushed vibe can stick with you all day long, influencing everything you do. When you change this habit, you change the game!

Now, you're smart enough to know that there's no point having a wonderful sleeping routine if your bed sleeping situation, is crap. You need a comfortable bed with a decent mattress, pillow, clean sheets.

Sleep is *essential*. We all need a good night's sleep. This is how we recharge our body and clean it up from whatever was going on the day before. We need to refresh, so that we can attack another day.

This brings me to the second tip:

2. Sleep Meditation:

For those who work night shifts or in the evenings this is particularly important! Sleep meditation is the best thing that has happened to me. I repeat, **sleep meditation is the best thing to happen to me!** Yes, I needed to shout that out.

It took me time to realize its benefits.

Like all good things. But as soon as I did, whoa mama! I really felt different. The best part of it is... wait for it...**You don't need to do shit**! Besides sleeping, that is. The mind does *everything* for you!

There are so many good sleeping meditation videos out there, but I'll save you the searching and give you a list of what I use. If you don't feel a difference in a month, then change it up and try another one that might work better for you. Same species — all different.

Check out some of my favorites here: https://youtube.com/@FYPFuckYourPast

Try saying this beauty before sleeping:

"Loving God and Tender Shepherd, please hear my cry for help with the struggles and difficulties in my life. I confess that all too often I have tried to handle them alone. I know I cannot face these difficulties without your help, grace, and power. Please bless me with these today."

3. Say a few words before bed and when you wake up:

Before I go to sleep and while the meditation music or sound is playing, I usually thank God* for what I have and share my fears. After I've talked everything through, I say, "Thank you for my fears. I choose love instead." This way I can face and let go of my fears which has made a huge difference to me.

It sounds too easy, right? Believe me, letting go of anything in life is hard. Gee, even letting go of old clothes is hard for most of us! I know someone who bought a new TV. She put the old one in her car, planning to donate it to charity. She drove around with that TV in the back of her car for so long! But she couldn't let it go...

We make excuses, saying something like, "I'll just leave it in the closet. I might need it one day." You know that useless stuff holds us down, so get rid of it! Why not give it to someone who will wear it instead of letting it rot in the closet? That's why I choose to speak to my fears before going to bed. I know that once I've let go of them, the sleeping meditation will do the rest of the work for me.

Then, when I wake, I say, "Thank you, God*, for my life and for returning my soul to me with great passion."

*Note: Here you may wish to thank the universe or whatever else that feels right to you. It's just about being grateful.

After this small prayer, I thank God for:

- Morning light/sunshine.
- Nature.
- The gift of life.
- My family's love and support.
- Those around me.
- The opportunities I already have and will have today.
- Self-love and attracting new love into my life.
- The ability to forgive myself for the bad choices I've made.

- The ability to forgive those who let me down.
- The ability to live my dream life.
- For all my blessings.
- The ability to trust and be trusted.
- That which is.

Finally, before I get out of bed, I stretch my body.

Chapter Six: The Basics of Manifestation

How can you manifest what you want to bring into your life? Get a clear understanding of what you want.

- Ask the universe.
- Work toward your goals and start believing in your abilities.
- Aim high but start with what you can do for now. Movement and energy are what we want.
- Trust the process.
- Receive and acknowledge what comes to you, and don't forget what you already have.
- Keep your vibration high.

- Clear your resistance/fears and thank those thoughts instead of fighting them.
- Choose love over negativity, look at the positive and let go.
- Remember - you got this!

Over the course of my life, I've always been very spiritual, but in my own way. I have always believed in God and observed all the traditions and holidays. At the same time, I had so many questions, most of all, wondering about our existence in this world. I knew I had a purpose. We all do, but I was having a really hard time finding it! I know many of you can relate.

Until Covid appeared, then the whole world paused for a second. It had to! We were forced to stop and reevaluate. Covid has affected us all in such varied ways.

For me, the unknown became clearer. I took a good look at my past in order to find the answers to my questions. What I discovered was huge. I realized what I was doing wrong, figured out a way to change it, and during the process, realized something very simple. All my life, I seemed to be sacrificing something to achieve something. That was my mindset. Although I understood the reason for sacrificing, it always brought me back to the story of Jacob and Isaac, where God asked Jacob to sacrifice his son.

I was thinking about how far Jacob would go for his belief in God. I spent time reflecting on that story during those days, as well as the story of Adam and Eve. So many questions came to my mind:

- Are we really in hell right now?
- Are we suffering because of our fathers?

"אבות אכלו בוסר ושני בנים תקהינה"

- Which means. "The fathers have eaten sour grapes, and the children's teeth are set on edge." In other words, children will suffer for their parents' misdeeds.
- Will we ever learn from our father's mistakes and find peace within ourselves, and not get thrown into hell repeatedly?
- *When* will we learn?

There were many other questions that swirled around my head during this time, as I'm sure they did for you too. It all got me thinking — are we here to make a deal with God, or to get what we want, do we need to make a deal with the Monkey mind (or Devil)?

The concept of sacrifice in order to get what you want sounds like a deal with the Monkey (or Devil) who comes to you and asks what is it you really want? What is it you desire? And what are you willing to do for it? This is the mindset I've grown up with.

Think about it. In general, in life, you make sacrifices. Say you want to lose weight or build muscles. You sacrifice your body to get results. You sacrifice time spent at the gym instead of going out.

Now, the more you sacrifice, the bigger the results, right? For example, if you want to have a fit body, you need a mix of twice-daily gym sessions, combined with a strict diet. So, without knowing it, daily, you are making so many sacrifices for a "fit" result.

You're sacrificing:

- Meals
- Your health - the possibility of getting injured during workouts.
- The possibility of being sore after a workout.
- And most importantly, Time!

These are just a few things that pop into my mind, but you get the idea.

So how do you know whether your sacrifices are a deal with the Monkey or your Monk? How can you tell if your life struggles are indeed a gift? Well, life struggles became a gift to me when I shifted my perspective. When I look back at my life, all those hard times I went through as a child, and then as an adult when I failed repeatedly, I see how it all shaped me into who I am today.

It took longer than I expected to get past the pain, the regrets, the blaming and so on. But that was time well spent to get me to where I needed to be. As soon as you can find your purpose, you will find your own meaning in life. That's when everything changes. You'll be able to see things differently and appreciate life and what you have. You will be able to control your thoughts and understand what is good or bad, whether it's the Monkey speaking or your Monk. You will be able to get out of bed early!

Let's take, for example, the time I was using drugs because I thought it was fun. I didn't realize how much damage it was doing to me mentally. I knew that drugs were bad for my health. Everyone knows it. But I never really thought that the side effects could last more than a day or two, which I thought was worth it.

However, those side effects lasted more than that. A lot more. They became my daily reality. So, even though I wasn't using daily, just once or twice a week, the impact they made on my life lasted years.

Now I know that those who are using any kind of drugs are just trying to escape. In fact, instead of getting away from their troubles, they're really doing the opposite. It makes everything worse! Drug users are people just like me, who have suffered and if they keep going this way, they will suffer for the rest of their lives. Don't let this be you!

When I realized the effect, the drugs were having on me (and it took some time because I truly was in denial), I decided to quit. My reality instantly changed for the better. What makes it more beautiful though, is that my struggle through all of that made me who I am today. Guys, it's hard to see now, but you will come out of your struggles *grateful* for how they have made you who you are.

Sharing this with you, I am so full of hope that you will make these changes, find your purpose, and create a happier life. Your success will be my fulfillment and success!

There is so much light inside your struggles, the good in the bad, even if you can't see it right now. It's up to you to choose to see it that way, no one can make that choice for you. I can help lead you there, but it's you, buddy, who has to make that choice. When it comes to this, there is only black and white. There is only the Monkey or the Monk. If you choose your Monk, you will be able to change your reality. If you choose your Monkey, you choose to stay where you are, or even worse, go backward. Be aware of what you are always choosing. Don't make thoughtless choices. Always think, am I choosing the Monkey's way or the Monk's way?

Chapter Seven: Let's Make Better Choice

I personally feel that those who choose money over a meaningful purpose in life, a purpose that helps others, or the planet, are making a deal with the Monkey. If they are using their money to control other people instead of helping them, well, they are stuck in the Adam and Eve mindset of, "Take what we can, leave nothing for anyone but ourselves." They don't care about the outcome of their actions, they only care for their own personal satisfaction.

On the other hand, those who get rich/successful and return to those who helped them along the way, or help those in need, they're making a deal with the Monk.

A generous person is recognized not by their money, but by simple daily acts such as opening a door to someone else, or buying a coffee for the person behind you, without motive of course. It is tipping for service or giving to a homeless person without caring what he does with the money.

These small gestures mean more than you think. They can deliver great hope! There are many gestures too, that don't cost you a thing, like smiling at one another and saying "Hi" to people you don't necessarily know. Did you know how invisible the elderly feel? A smile can make their day! These gestures, these small actions show us whether this is a person who chooses to live the Monk way or the Monkey way.

It is all about choices and being *aware* that you have choices!

Repeat after me:

- I choose to be here.
- I choose to embrace this world.
- I choose to read this book.
- I choose to be happy today.
- I choose to smile at passersby.
- I choose to be with my family and friends.
- I choose to make good or bad choices.
- I choose to put myself in bad situations.
- I choose to get out of bad situations.
- I choose to change my habits.
- I choose to work on myself before helping others (and in order to help others).

- I choose to help others because I want to do good, not for the benefit of getting something from that person.
- I choose to listen to the Monk.

Remember, no one is putting a gun to your head every day. We all have a choice but for some reason, we choose not to be happy, we choose to be stressed. Yes, life can be stressful, and hard, but it doesn't mean it has to stay this way.

It might take some hard work. But hard can be good. Like when you are climbing a mountain it's not easy. But in the end, we reach the peak, and take in that amazing view! That is how life works and it's a choice if you want to climb this mountain or not. It's a choice to stay miserable due to events that have happened to you.

YOUR CHOICE! So many have suffered the most horrific situations, and have made the choice to be happy, to not let things cloud their every day.

All the situations you have got yourself into in the past are no one's fault but your own. So, own them. Let go of blaming other people for what happened to you, or for how they make you feel.

No one has the power to make you feel anything. It's your choice to how you respond, how you react. They didn't force you to do something or feel a certain way. You may have been influenced, pressured, and so on. Or people may be cruel, or thoughtless, or treat you unkindly due to their own issues. But it's YOU that has chosen how to react. There *were* times when you could have said NO! Or even, HELL NO!! Or the best one F.CK NO!!!

There were times when you could have not taken something to heart. You could have chosen to stand strong, to let yourself not be vulnerable to words or actions that hurt you. To not take to heart every unkind thing said about you because no matter who you are, it happens. It's always your choice to have a thick or thin skin.

For example, there are those who have a dog, like me, who have decided to leave our dogs in the apartment by themselves and trust them to not do something stupid like eating our favorite shoes. So, we make sure we leave the shoes somewhere safe, thinking, *she won't be able to get to them here*. We return home and catch her with the shoe inside her mouth, head turned sideways, looking so cute but at the same time your expensive shoe is in her mouth! We flip out and start screaming

"NOOOOOO!!!" And put the dog in her home space/cage for punishment.

But if we look at the big picture, is it really the dog's fault? Did she leave the shoes behind? Did we not know it could have happened if we left the shoes out instead of somewhere safe?

I'm sure by now you get my point. It is time we stopped blaming others for past issues and present hurts. It is 100% our choice in life. If you can take full responsibility for your actions, you can easily brush off failure or any other kind of bad results. Think how much easier it is to say, okay, that was my fault for that action or feeling hurt by what someone said. How quickly can we move on? When we get stuck in blaming others for our pain, it eats away at us. Take responsibility, stop blaming others, and you will be able to build yourself up quicker, snap out of pain and hurt, and fix it so that next time you are going to put the shoes in the closet/ignore the hurtful comments or actions, and move on with your happy day. There will always be hurtful people whether they mean it or not, hurtful actions and disappointments, for none of us are perfect. Not even you! Hell no, you're not!!

Climb that mountain, guys; the view will be worth it!

4. Meditate/Pray as you wake up:

Every morning I pray. There are a few prayers I say when I wake up, as well as throughout the day. Praying to a source of energy keeps you grounded, as does meditation. That is why I do both daily.

You can pray or meditate at any given time of day, but the best time is during the morning when you just open your eyes and thank God/the universe for bringing back your soul to your body. This is what I say every morning:

"Thank you for this day, thank you for the air I breathe, thank you for the gift of life."

Let's try to find what words of prayer fit you. Remember, the good thing about praying is you can pray for any kind of reason (happiness, sadness, or asking for help). Prayer isn't a ritual that depends on closing our eyes and putting on holy faces! We don't have to kneel or sit. We can pray while walking, driving, or working. God/the universe can respond to a cry for help in the middle of a busy afternoon, just like He does so at a focused prayer time, or after reading scripture in the morning. Praying doesn't have to be complicated. God delights in any simple words we offer Him.

So, let's find a prayer that feeds you. It can be anything that resonates with you. It could be something that your mom or dad or grandma/grandpa used to say, or maybe something that you heard and felt connected to like I did. It may be based on Buddhism or a simple philosophy. I have a few different prayers I use at different times and situations. These prayers help me throughout the day, sometimes I even say them for no reason, just to bring awareness to my life, my goals, and my higher self.

Maybe these prayers will help you too:

"Thank you, God, for your ever-present sanctuary of love and joy and peace within my heart. My only need is to savor your sweet presence in my life. I truly trust – that I am in your care, and all is well."
"Thank you, God. Thank you, for your living truth as it speaks to me in unmistakable ways. I am still my body. I am still my mind. I relax completely. I surrender myself to
You, God. Fill me with your presence as I listen in silence."

"Holy Presence within me, I am willing to release all feelings of hurt and anger and resentment. Help me know true forgiveness and see each person as part of you. Let my words and my actions serve only to glorify

you. May they heal and comfort and harmonize my life and the lives of those around me. Thank You, God."

"Great Spirit of this Universe, how glorious are your ways. My human mind cannot fully grasp the magnitude of all that you are, yet I know I am yours. Thank you for the safety of your guiding presence — wherever I am, whatever I do."

"Thank you, God, for the growing awareness of who I am. You have created me to express you. I make the commitment today to be your hands, your voice, your heart. Live your life through me — fully and completely. The cells of my body shout for joy as they resurrect into new life!"

"Thank you, God, for your powerful healing presence as it touches every atom of my body, calling forth a radiant wholeness. I choose this day to love over fear."

Again, you should remember what I'm about to say is no magic trick! As I've mentioned before, "God helps those who help themselves." If you're going to start praying just because I said so, it will not serve the purpose. You need to be one hundred percent into it with the understanding that it may take time, but that this small step will make this energy respond. It could be on the same day, it could take days, weeks, or months. If you keep going and believe that it will, there is nothing there to stop it. It will become your reality! But any small doubts can mess it up.

I remember having a feeling that my ex would contact me. But then as soon as I doubted it or started to think about our past this feeling of her coming back was still there, but it took her two years to finally step up and call me. She explained what really happened and it really helped me to find closure. I believe that those thoughts and doubts are what made this closure take longer than expected. The same doubts I had over success meant that success came late for me too. Or maybe it came at the right time, which is also possible. The fact that I was not ready for success because of the way I was living my life, meant that it took longer.

Now, let's chat about meditation, my favorite thing in the world! It's a real game-changer for me. If you love yoga that will help too, but for me, I prefer meditation.

I feel it's more powerful and feeds the purpose, not to mention you can do this on your own, no need to pay anyone to teach you each week. Thank God for YouTube! But really, how lucky we are to have such wonderful resources at our fingertips. And it's thanks to the generous souls that share their knowledge, too.

So, is meditation for you? It took me some time to find the right meditation. Even though I'm going to share with you my meditation, it may not work for you. Keep looking until you find one, you're happy with.

It's not easy to explain the benefits of meditation. Actually, I find it really tricky! Instead, I prefer to talk about how it makes me feel. How are you supposed to feel in meditation? And what do you need to do to feel or enjoy meditation?

Meditation is a practice where an individual uses a technique — such as mindfulness or focusing the mind on a particular object, thought, or activity — to train attention and awareness, and achieve a mentally clear, emotionally calm, and stable state. The result of this calm and stable state: greater happiness. Meditation can increase your levels of feel-good chemicals, like endorphins and serotonin. Studies also indicate that meditation may increase your capacity for happiness and reduce your propensity towards negativity.

While meditating, it's natural that you may feel random aches, feel itchy or tingly at the start of the session. The body feels the mind's frustrations, and you may want to stand up or even give up. It's uncomfortable. At times you may become tired, with your body feeling heavy, sleepy, or sluggish. You may also feel restless, that you're wasting time, that you should be doing something more "important" but truly, there is nothing more important than training your mind.

The main idea behind meditation is to relax your "monkey mind" which is overthinking, and we achieve this by using simple breathing techniques. We want to quieten the Monkey's thoughts – which will really try to pop up now! The Monkey might say things like, "You're hopeless at this," or, "This is a waste of time," or, "Who do you think you are, meditating?" or, "My back hurts, my legs hurt," or "I'm hungry, tired, thirsty..." and so on. You've got to ignore him!

Can you imagine what the Monk might say if she was a little louder than the Monkey? She'd say something like,

"You've got this, keep trying," or, "Good on you for trying meditation!" or, "You really are getting your life on track," or, "I'm proud of you..."

What most people forget to explain, is how to avoid this monkey mind being a cheeky, annoying monkey, and how exactly can we control the guy? We control the monkey mind by not *forcing* ourselves to control it. In order not to force control, which only leads to added frustration, you need to focus on the breath. How? Say to yourself:

"Breathe in, hold your breath"

"Breathe out and release all tension."

So, let's try it:

- Find a comfortable position, sitting or lying down on the floor, back straight. The bottom of your body should be relaxed and connected to the surface you are sitting or lying on. Take a moment to feel the surface beneath you.
- Take a deep breath and say, "Breathe in."
- Hold your breath, and slowly count: "1-2-3-4-5."
- Breathe out and release all tension.

Repeat this multiple times. Don't worry about any thoughts that pop into your head, and don't fight them. Let them be, keep counting, breathing, and letting them go. If you've never tried meditating before, you will realize how busy, crammed and incessant the mind can be. Just how crazy that monkey is! You'll see just how unfriendly he can be. How damn pesky! He really needs to calm the f.ck down.

Let me share a trick that will help you get used to it that little bit faster and might even make those monkey thoughts go away completely.

- While taking a deep breath, I want you to *crunch* your stomach hard, like you are holding everything inside of you. As you hold everything, (your breath and stomach), you will feel like you are taking everything in and about to lose your breath. Don't! Not yet.
- Count "1-2-3-4-5," then release the air and tension from your body.
- This action will make you feel like you have released all stress and will

make you feel like letting go. You will feel relief with every bit of air you release.

- Once you get the hang of this, I want you to incorporate some intentional thoughts. Think of whatever you want to manifest into your life, or any stress you want to let go, and out of your life.
- Keep the focus on one thing at a time.

Engaging in this technique over time, will help you control your thoughts, and later you will not need to spend so much effort to stop the thoughts. Your mind will be more skilled at this process, and you will be able to simply breathe in, and out in a more relaxed way. Not to mention being more able to focus on manifesting good things into your life or letting go.

Check out a few of my favorite meditations here. All of them brought miracles into my life: https://youtube. com/@FYPFuckYourPast

Mary Kate's meditation on YouTube is one of my absolute favorites. She also has some cool sleep meditations, and many others that you may find useful.

Now, that I've shared my meditation options, what do you prefer? A male or female voice?

Or simply relaxing sounds? Try a few things, keep an open mind, and good luck!

Alright, so meditation is one of my favorite things. Do you want to know another one of my favorite things. Pets! I love them so much, but most of all I love dogs. One of the reasons I love dogs so much is their loyalty. Everyone knows how loyal, loving, and friendly they are.

What is truly fascinating about dogs is their ability to live in the moment. They take us to the moment too. They help us slow down, and literally smell the roses — don't they just sniff everything?!

Dogs are never stuck in the past, never stuck in regret, or resentments. They do learn in all kinds of different ways what we like or don't like them to do, like when to sit, pee and poop outside and not eat our furniture. The list goes on. They *never* hold a grudge. The next day, after being troublesome they just act as if nothing happened. As soon as you walk up and say, "Hey Buddy!" they act like they haven't seen you in days. They are just SO happy to see you. This ability to not be stuck in the past and live in the moment is what makes dogs so happy and fun. It's also what makes them heal so fast from physical or emotional situations in their lives.

Once, I took my dog to a spay surgery. Seeing her after the surgery was hard for me. It was also hard for me to sleep. Any noise she made would wake me up. I was so protective of her, following the doctor's guidelines, keeping her distance from other dogs, not letting her run or go to the park, etc. As I was watching her, I realized that the next day she was acting like nothing happened to her. Yes, she made a few whimpering noises of suffering at times, but very small. The way she dealt with her pain was to act as if it wasn't there. Her progress of healing was *so* quick as a result. Even her stitches and the cut on her belly was healing in a way that really surprised me.

I told my cousin, who loves animals and has studied them closely. Her reply: "What's good about dogs, is that they do not feel sorry for themselves, unlike us. Because she lives in the moment, and not in the past. She recovers quickly."

This is also true of our own process of self-healing. If we want to heal and enjoy life, we need to live in the present. It's all we have, guys. It's the key to life. Without letting go of the past you can't live the present, you can't enjoy the beautiful moments of *now*, and you can't really plan the future.

Always be aware of where you are now. Are you stuck in the past, way back in the past? Or still stewing on something that happened yesterday? Or are you caught up in worrying over the future or thinking the future is when you will be happy? The mind, heart, and spirit need to be connected just like the past, present and future. All need to be in alignment. Our mind needs to be honest with ourselves. It needs to be aware -- Are we listening to the Monkey or the Monk? Are we in the past, present, or future? We need to listen to our hearts and minds, to be able to let go of the Monkey, the monkey mind, the negativity.

When we can connect the mind and heart, we can more easily let go of the

Monkey mindset, the temptations. You will be amazed at what you can achieve. And meditation will help with that.

These days, I'm more aware of where I'm at because my heart and mind are more aligned. I have more energy and purpose, and I'm also able to do "less" and gain more.

Me doing less doesn't necessarily mean that I stop working or doing less while I'm at work.

I just manage my time in such a way that I ensure I spend four-five hours focused on things I should do to improve my company and I give it my 100%.

The rest of the day I spend on keeping my body and mind healthy, learning new things, and enjoying my life. I mean we've all heard people say that every day we should learn something new, try a new experience, keep the mind and brain active, blah blah blah, but the question is — how can I do this if I'm working the same job that takes up most of my day (including travel time etc.) doing the same old thing, and having no time or energy left to do anything more.

Well, I hear it a lot. It's hard to fit everything in, but even reading a helpful book can make all the difference. A few pages a day, and it will all add up to new insights, a new life.

And just because you've read one book on one topic, doesn't mean you can't read many more on that topic that inspires or interests you. There are so many points of view and little things you can learn.

Let's go back to my dear dog, Shelly, for a moment. (Her stage name is Chanel!) Gee, I love her. I adopted her because I felt

I needed a loyal friend in my life. I cannot begin to list the number of things she has helped me with. I'm just so thankful for her. I didn't save her; she saved me with her loving spirit and ability to live her life in the moment. I learn more about myself when I'm with her, more than I can admit. Even though she can't read this book, I thank her for being in my life!

How can we tap into the incredible way dogs live their lives? For us humans, it seems an impossible task. How can you compare dogs, who have no real challenges, worries, or stress, when their daily routine is to sleep, play, eat, pee, and poop? That's it!

But that's not 100% right. They are very emotional creatures, yet still, they have the ability to live in the moment and are not consumed by the past like we are.

They also adapt to their environment very quickly. They are intelligent, and after a few lessons learning the difference between good and bad, they can change their habits. They learn from their mistakes, knowing that if they pee in the house, they will be notified by their owner not to do it again. Why do they do this? The key thing here is that the dog wants to change his habits out of his love for his owner. It's like the idea behind a habit is the reward that one gets from doing it. For example, when we are hungry the habit that comes with that is to eat. Our reward is satisfying that hunger. Our dog's reward for behaving well is lots of pats and cuddles! Or maybe even a tasty treat.

For some of us, if we feel miserable with our lives, we tend to reward ourselves with bad habits, such as over-eating, drinking, smoking, drugs, spending money, etc., thinking that those things will make the situation better. We all know it doesn't. In order to change those bad habits, we should be motivated to change.

For example, to change a dog's bad habit there are a few ways to do this, the most common one being to give the dog a treat when he does the right thing. Let's look at the big picture of the idea behind this. The dog pees outside, which is a good thing, and he gets good rewards. These good rewards encourage him to do the same thing frequently. This is how you change bad habits into good habits.

Gradually as I changed myself, I listed all the things I love doing and that which gives me real joy. I was amazed to find out that all the things that I really enjoy the most, were simple stuff; and most of them were from my childhood.

Like riding my bicycle, it took me back to feeling like a teenager, going to school or basketball training, and meeting my friends. So, now every time I get the chance to ride, I do it. And it feels great! *And* it improves my whole day.

It's the same with going to the gym, reading a book, meditating, walking along the pier, spending time with my family and of course my dog, listening to music, watching movies at home or the cinema, and playing sports.

So, let's try to figure out what you truly love to do? And help you make time for DOING WHAT YOU LOVE.

5. What will you choose?

I want to start this step by asking you to say this:

- I choose to be happy.
- I choose to see my situation with love.
- I choose to see my past with love.
- I choose to forgive myself.
- I choose to forgive those who let me down.
- I choose love over fear.
- I choose to share my happiness.
- I choose to share my wealth.
- I choose to help others.
- I choose to think these thoughts.
- I choose to enjoy my life from now on until the end of my life.
- I CHOOSE LOVE.

Memorize this and say it every day as you go about your day. Or when your day is not going your way add, "I choose to" whatever it is that is bothering you. This helps take ownership of your current actions and helps remind you that no one is forcing you to do whatever it is you are doing right now. The more you repeat this, the more it will pop up in your head and boost you throughout the day. Hopefully, like one of those pesky songs you can't get out of your head! You will begin to feel better and see changes throughout your day. By choosing to see any situation as a "choice" rather than ruminating in blame, we immediately change our mindset to a more positive one, especially, if the situation is bad. Say, "I choose to see this situation with love," instead of blaming yourself or others. It helps to remind yourself that it's okay, things happen, I can't change it now. Therefore, I choose to see this with love so I can move on with the rest of my day, or life. If you put faith in your hands and take responsibility for any situation in life, you will be able to pass through any kind of wall or situation brought on by that Monkey. You'll be able to hear the Monk's voice of reason. Try to build your, "I choose to...." list and work your way up to "I choose love over fear..." and include any others that you feel will benefit you.

If you choose to see difficult, upsetting, unpleasant, uncomfortable things with love, or simply "as they are," repeatedly, you will see a shift in your life. You are choosing to do what you are doing and not because you "have to!" This creates a huge shift. There's so much irritation, anger and blame caught up in "have to."

There is only one thing we "HAVE TO DO" ... and that is to die. We can't cheat death, but we have plenty of other choices. I want you to start removing these negative words out of your life. They are just so heavy! Things like, "need to, must do, can't do, should do."

Guys, be aware of what you are telling yourself. Be vigilant. If we simply change these words around to "I choose to," and "I want to," and, "It's my choice to," you can change your mood from being anxious, stressed, and overwhelmed to being calmer and in control. Those negative words simply f.ck with our minds. They are the Monkey's talk, right? Trying to make us think we don't have any other choice than to do this or that which we don't like, then we feel immense pressure, and we are unpleasant to be around too! It can lead us to making the wrong decisions or upset loved ones when we use blame.

Now in life, I know that sometimes we do have only one choice to make. But if we can try our best to use this choice as an "I choose to" instead of a "have to", over time we will turn that bad situation into a better one, as we try hard to see the good instead of the bad.

Trust me when I say this, it's not easy! And that is because we are so used to the "need/have to" mindset, and I still make the same mistake. It's the practice that helps cement the new mindset, and you know what? All you need to do is be aware that you made a mistake and correct it. You will still see a big shift in your energy as soon as you change the wording. Be aware, be vigilant because if we keep saying those negative words it will become our reality;

we will attract those bad situations often we will find ourselves even cursing people for the things we "have to" do.

Here is a funny way to "curse" people, when someone has changed my mood. I usually "curse" them saying, "health." Now, usually, people think I'm the crazy one or have trouble with my English, but in my head this person is not healthy, so better to say to him to be healthy than "cursing" him nastily with a "Karma is a bitch, buddy." The thing is karma will be a bitch and your cursing will not serve you well either! Keep cool!

We are all human — happy people or good people get upset too. If you change your life to incorporate good habits, it doesn't mean that you can't get upset, or that your ego will not be there. It's okay if you're aware, correct it, and "choose to see this situation with love," instead. It's awareness that allows us to correct things.

Listening to the Monkey's words or the Monk's is a very important step for a better life. When we understand that we have a choice in our lives, we choose to come from a place of understanding or happiness wherever possible, that's when it will change everything in our lives.

You might not see an immediate effect or change, but I guarantee that over time when those changes of words become automatic, you will see and feel differently.

Do you remember how hard it was to drive a car at first? And once you got it, and practiced, it became effortless. Let's aim for that! How good would it be...?!You will feel yourself letting go of so many bad situations, or even unnecessary irritations, due to being aware, and making that change.

Not long ago I was living my life in the sort of standard way. I had a secure job, had lots of friends, and I was enjoying life. However, during that time, I was barely making my rent and bill payments like so many others. It's not easy! I just thought this was normal life. I thought, I will just work hard, show my worth, give 100% and ask for a raise, and things will get better. As I was going on with my life, I saw my friends getting rich while I was stuck in the same loop, over and over again. The day I found myself sleeping in a van, I decided to make a change.

It wasn't easy. None of this stuff is. I even thought that I was on the right track, but again I had had a big fallout. After three years of good production, for some reason, I was still not able to make it. It wasn't until I started to dig into my past in order to find the reason for my failures, that my life truly turned around.

I was so amazed to find out that my issues were so deep that they had become my reality. So much so that it just felt normal to me. You see though, over the course of our lives we are adding layers of new habits. Those deep ones are hard to see or even realize they are there. Again, it's all about awareness. How the hell can we fix anything without being aware?

Most of the additional habits are usually bad ones, such as drinking or finding other ways to "let go" and "feel free" of our daily troubles, or more correctly, escaping the reality we are living, and blaming everyone else but ourselves. So, I made a choice, a choice that you can make too.

This choice to change your life is a hard choice to make. It means starting fresh and possibly being alone with yourself while you figure things out, while you take a step back to reevaluate what's important and what you want to do and who you want in your life. It may be that a dog or a cat will be your only company until you get your sh.t together, and that is cool! We need space to hear ourselves, to be aware, to slow down and hear what our soul wants and needs. Pet cuddles go a long way too for comfort, cheer, and companionship. I highly recommend you get a furry friend!

This choice to change your life means not being afraid, it means betting on yourself, believing in yourself and most importantly, forgiving yourself. All the while - listening to the quieter Monk and ignoring the loud pesky Monkey.

You truly are the only one who made the choice to be where you are right now, and so only you can be the only one to shift that around. Your friends or family didn't hold a gun to your head all the time up until this point in your life.

It's also time to let go of those who are holding you back, those who keep lying to you, those who pretend to be there but are not when you really need them, those who make you feel bad especially when you are doing so good. Those who aren't supportive of your moves or decisions. Those who want to keep you down with them, for they are afraid they will lose you if you rise. That's not a true friend, and besides, you can't help them when you are both down.

Being alone is part of the healing process, and many of those who have walked the path of self-change before you, have done so alone. If you can't be by yourself, you will always follow the wrong people. You will never have a stand or a say and you will not take responsibility for your actions, blaming everyone else but yourself. People will keep stepping on you repeatedly if they can.

I let go of everyone around me for a time, even my family. I kept in touch a few times a week perhaps, to let them know I'm okay. It wouldn't be fair on close loved ones to leave them wondering if I'm doing alright! Without the support of my family, I'm not sure I would be able to be where I'm right now. Which is funny when I look at my past and my life which I'm grateful for, the bad and the good. It was always my family that kept me strong, and the bond just got stronger over the years.

Perhaps as a kid, you thought you had a hard-knock life, and you are ashamed or afraid someone will find out, so as a kid you tried to pretend that things were normal in your life just to fit into the system or friend group? As we grow older and hear other people's stories about how they too have struggled, each in different ways, we begin to realize that struggles are a normal part of life. It's how we deal with them that matters. When we are younger, we tend to blame others for our struggles, our parents, upbringing, etc., but as we age, we know that no life is perfect and that parents are human too and did their best they could at the time. Ninety percent of people in society have their own struggles and can share a story or two!

Struggle is not bad! It's what makes us who we are right now. It's why you are reading books like this to find answers to your issues and to figure out how to change, mend those issues and embrace the future. That is why I think and feel we are kind of living in a Monkey world, where we ruminate, blame, and are attracted to the negative. However, we can climb up from here to live a life of love, being grateful for what we have, and sharing it with those who we love or finding new love and new friends. It will be a new life because you are realizing what is important. You're becoming aware of what you need and want. Are you excited? C'mon, you must be!

Okay, so let's go back to the idea of changing our habits. When I realized how deep I needed to dig in order to understand my issues, the world stopped. And when I say the world stopped, it really did. Covid-19 had just arrived. NYC was shut down, so I had nowhere to go and nothing to do, besides facing those issues. Yikes! But the social distancing did me good (I do apologize in advance if you lost someone during this time, and if this time was truly horrific for you, as I know it was for many). At this time, I had just started my company and didn't have enough work to hold me for a full year. I was stressed. Stressed to the point where I noticed I was losing hair in parts of my body that I didn't even think was possible to lose — my chin! So, instead of carrying on in this way, I chose instead to make a change, face my fears and issues. Slowly, and at my own pace, and alone! All the steps I shared with you led me to those changes. At the end of this hard time, I finally had:

- No fear of how I was going to pay my rent.
- No fear of how I would pay my bills.
- No fear of how much food I could buy, and what kind of lease I had.
- No fear of wondering what I could and couldn't afford right now.
- No fear of adopting a dog and wondering whether I would be able to maintain taking care of her too?

It took me eight to nine months to feel free. I don't mean fully accomplishing my dreams, because my dreams are big and were big at the time. I felt free of those fears to a big extent. That awful feeling of needing to calculate in my head the expenses of everything was slowly vanishing from my mind. I used to be so careful of where I would buy groceries and what I could afford to buy to not feel hungry. I'm now at the point of not looking at the prices so carefully anymore! A good feeling! And I want you to be able to feel the same.

If you can appreciate the small things along this initial slow process, you are in the right direction. Only you can see and define your happiness by these small changes, these small (but truly big changes). Only you can know when you feel fulfilled and can enjoy the rest of your life. Each of us has our own idea of a dream life, and as you know my dream life may be even smaller than yours or bigger, it doesn't really matter. As long as you are happy with yourself and with what you are achieving with every part of your body, physically, soulfully, and mentally.

Such as doing good things once a day for example. Every morning like most of us I go to the same coffee spot near my building. Once there was a man in front of me who was about to order a croissant. As soon as he opened his wallet and saw the price, he changed his mind. I know the girl in front, so I ask her to call him back and tell him I will take care of his order. On my way out he thanked me. I smiled and said, "Sure thing, enjoy." I went on with my day, stopping at the bus station near the coffee place, waiting for the driver. Guess what happened? The driver of the bus was the guy I had just bought the croissant for. He took care of the bus ticket, which he didn't really need to because I had a monthly pass, but that is not the point. The point is you never know what can happen in your day from doing something good for someone else without expecting something in return. Remember: "God gives to those who give to themselves." This story is an example of that.

6. How to get rid of an old habit:

If you do not already know which habits are good or bad for you, make a list of your daily routine, for example:

- I wake up at...
- As soon as I wake up, I think...
- I take a shower
- I brush my teeth
- I get ready to go to work

- I arrive at my destination at....
  (Early? late?)

And so, the list goes on...

Now:
- Write one list of an example of a good day — a day where you felt the day started well, you felt happy, calm, and in control.
- Next, write a list of a stressful day — a day where you felt it just went all wrong, starting from the get-go.
- Lastly, write a list for a typical weekend of activities you enjoy, that brings you some chance to recharge and some real enjoyment.

As soon as you have completed this, you will easily be able to identify the habits that are damaging your performance, and the ones that boost your performance. I mean we always have bad days that we just cannot control. What we can control is the little things to get our days off to a better start, all the way through and even the way we end the day. Try to analyze the lists in a way that makes sense to you. It is amazing how lists can really help clarify what's going on in your life.

You need to understand that old habits are like body fat! For us to get rid of it, we will need to try lots of diets until we find the one that works for us and makes us happy. We need to find out what gives us the results we want on any given day. We all know how it is to lose weight, but when we are seeing the progress of a diet, seeing our body thinning out and feeling healthier, more energy, the feeling of satisfaction, confidence, and happiness will be worth the process. You'll see and feel that all the hard work to get to the end goal will be worth your while.

Changing old habits is not easy! Don't I know it? But the feeling of being able to change them is worth every hard day of changing it. For example, there are two ways to get rid of unwanted fat:

- Surgery
- Work that takes time.

The difference between the two is that surgery is the easy way. In life, we know that when we cut corners, we usually end up losing. Those who decide to take the shortcut, without changing their habit, will go back to being fat. Whoever chooses to do the work that takes time, will most likely not gain that fat back. By choosing work and the time it takes, you are choosing the process and the idea of needing to change your habits. It's a mindset change that will give you lifetime results, not to mention the satisfaction and the confidence that results from that. Often, these things snowball too. The feeling that you *can* do something if you try, means you are more likely to try to change other habits too. Before you know it, you're making *life* changes, baby!

Let's go back to your lists. After making the list of habits, see if each habit benefits you or slows you down towards achieving your goals. If you have problems deciding which one is good or bad, then here are some questions that may help you. (In order to change habits, you need to be a self-detective, looking for those habits daily.)

Here we go:

- Does this habit help improve me?
- Does this habit make my life easier?
- Does this habit bring me closer to my goals, or does it slow me down?
- Will I benefit from changing this habit?
- Does this habit support the life that I want to have?

Remember, the secret of your future is hidden in your daily routine. I'm going to shout that one out because it's just SO important. You can't do amazing things by having a few amazing days. THE SECRET

OF YOUR FUTURE IS HIDDEN IN YOUR DAILY ROUTINE.

- If you want to be a writer, write a little (or a lot) every day.
- If you want to help others, help every day.
- If you want to learn, study every day.
- If you want to lose weight, exercise every day.
- If you want to be happier, smile every day.
- If you want healthy teeth, brush them every day.
- If you want a good relationship with your kids, spend time with your kids every day.

You get the idea!

I mentioned in my first book "FYP" that the best way to make a change is by taking small steps — because making those small adjustments every day makes a bigger challenge so much easier. That way, we won't feel too pressured, we won't feel overwhelmed, and we won't feel a sudden burst to quit. It's hard work, but we've got to be aware of those Monkey voices and listen carefully to our Monk. The Monkey is TOTALLY tempting you to quit! He'll say stuff like, "You'll never make it, who are you kidding?" and, "Ah, this is too hard, take a break." He is even very sneaky and will seduce you with comments like, "You can do it another time, go easy on yourself, you don't even really need to lose weight, you deserve a big treat..." and so on. Beware! Be Aware! Ignore the Monkey and listen to your Monk who is trying hard for you to hear her. She's saying, *WE CAN DO THIS, you're getting there, Step by step, I love you,* etc. So, start small and slowly, slowly those steps will become a habit.

Remember, your Monk knows you. You just need to remember to be aware of him, listen to him. Only you know what good and bad habits are and which need to change and how to go about that change.

Dr. Apj Abdul Kalam once said, *"You cannot change your future, but you can change your habits, and surely your habits will change your future."*

If you want to change your habits, the environment you live in should also probably change. Think carefully about your environment and who you surround yourself with because that is where we tend to pick up our habits. It could be where you live, your work environment, who you socialize with. How does your neighborhood environment influence your kids? Or their school? And here I'm talking about picking up not only bad habits, but good ones too.

As a teenager, if our group of friends smoked cigarettes or weed, we tended to try it too, and most likely, we'd pick up that habit. When I moved to NYC, I was around friends and their families who kept kosher food. Until then I used to keep my beliefs in God pretty much to myself and pray in my own way. It included praying in the morning and keeping the holidays only. I didn't really care if the chicken or beef was kosher or not, as long as it was not pork or shellfish. As soon as I met these families, I started to pick up their Jewish habits, which was Shabbat dinner on Fridays, then keeping kosher silverware, then kosher meat, and all without even realizing it!

When my brother moved to NYC and we decided to be roommates, he mixed his dishes with my kosher ones, and I got so mad! It was our first big fight. My brother eats everything, so it made things a bit tricky. He doesn't keep kosher and although he doesn't really believe in God, he does believe in an energy surrounding us.

Here is the funny part, some proof that we pick up habits from our surroundings. So. At one point in my life, I cut some friends from my life due to business reasons; they didn't support me partnering up with one of their subcontractors. During this time, I kept up the tradition of cooking and making my own Shabbat dinner with my brother, inviting my friends and occasionally, new ones joined us. We had about ten people over every Friday and had such a great time.

So how did this great habit of having a Shabbat dinner every Friday start? Well, my brother asked me when or if we were doing it again and if so, can he invite his new friends? Sure!

We both gained a lot from this, and you know what, this simple tradition has become his mantra! It's a way he and his kids choose to share the Jewish culture. He saw how this tradition united the family and brought them together in a positive way. So, you see, it's important to change your environment in order to change your habits. If something works, if something makes you feel great, try to make that a habit! Again, it comes back to being aware. Being aware of what makes you happy or unhappy.

I have kept up the Friday blessings, or dinner with either family or at the time I was living on my own, I did this just for me. It's about making the effort. I did go back to not caring if my chicken or beef was kosher because of who I am and what makes me happy, not to mention I try not to eat meat at all, but here and there I cheat on that part, and that's okay, isn't it?

The idea of changing habits will be that much easier if you are around people who have the same habits you would like to incorporate. You won't believe the influence of our friends, peers, and our environment — choose carefully!

Did you ever go to Australia or England and after a few days, you found yourself pronouncing words as they do, using the same accents they have? Or picking up little phrases? I started to say things like, "Oh Bloody Hell" or, "Fuck off" or my favorite, "Off you go then!" Lol.

It's all the same concept. Same-same, mate! So, adjust your environment in order to change your habits. It's as easy as that! Studies have shown that if you place your kid next to kids with a high IQ, your kid will eventually pick up, level up, and improve their IQ. Look at it this way, if we want to be a basketball player, we are going to copy our favorite player's moves, make them our own, then elevate our moves in our own way.

It's the same as observing successful people and how they behave, how they carry themselves, how they spend their time. How did they get there? Especially those who came from nothing. Reading biographies is a great motivation too. Although, we don't know those people personally, and can't be around them for them to rub their habits off on us (that would be great, wouldn't it?!) we can either read their books, follow news about them or watch lots of their videos, and learn what we can.

What do you think? How can you make changes to your environment? What steps will you take? Look for the simple answer, for the small step, because only small step leads to the bigger changes in life.

Be aware of adopting unhealthy habits from friends or family or taking on habits from a place of fear of their judgment. Make your own habits that make you feel good about yourself and where you are headed. As soon as you do that, you will attract more of your kind who like the same things as you, and appreciate you as you are, and not because you are doing something that you do not really want to do. They will see your energy; your passion and you'll attract like-minded people. You might feel it's selfish to create habits to make yourself happy, but really, remember; if you are not happy with yourself, you can't help others. So, if you want to help others, get your life together first! Doing something for someone else when you are not happy with your life, will leave you feeling lost, used, or judged. But when you are happy with yourself, you won't care what others think about you. And most likely those who judge you were not the ones that were going to be in your future life anyway.

Let's recap a little about our Monkey mind and delve a little deeper.

According to stories, (and Wikipedia!), the Monkey mind (Devil mind) is also known as Satan and is sometimes also called Lucifer in Christianity. It is a non-physical entity in the Abrahamic religions that seduces humans into sin or falsehood. In Judaism, Satan is seen as an agent subservient to God or typically regarded as a metaphor for the *yetzer hara*, or "evil inclination."

In Christianity and Islam, he is usually seen as either a fallen Monk or a jinni, who used to possess great piety and beauty but rebelled against God. Our conscience aside, we often go with the flow when it comes to having fun and enjoying our life. But how do we measure this open mind, (Monkey mind) our "*yetzer hara*?" Do we measure it by our circle of friends or family? What's normal around us or how society sees us if we do as we are not supposed to?

We often think that what we do is right because everyone else around us is doing it. But is it, really? Awareness, again, is key here. Being aware of what is right or wrong to us. We know, inside. Are we doing something to fit in because everyone does, or are we afraid to impress, or be pressured? Perhaps we are being brainwashed.

In traditional Judaism, the *yetzer hara* is not a demonic force, but rather man's misuse of things the physical body needs to survive. Thus, the need for food becomes gluttony due to the *yetzer hara*. The need for procreation becomes sexual abuse, and so on.

The idea behind the Monkey's mind is the idea of control. In the Jewish religion, this is not until the child reaches the age of thirteen for a boy and twelve for a girl. Until then, you're let off for not being able to control yourself, say, if you get into a fight or get into a bad situation, you're still just a kid. But as you get to the age of twelve or thirteen, you are old enough and should know by now the difference between good and bad, right and wrong. The idea behind the *yetzer hara* is to know how to control yourself.

For example, if you eat all day with no exercise, you know that in the end, you will get fat and maybe acquire some other health issues. Now eating is not a bad thing, but by this age, the fact is you know that eating too much is bad for you and you can control the habit or craving and are fully aware that the Monkey mind is telling you to "go on, eat it!"

This is a simple example of how it works, but it can also be from just stress or other emotions that means one is unable to control the Monkey mind, or simply out of habit from doing the same thing repeatedly, thinking and hoping things will change.

The only thing that is good to do over again is something that you know you will benefit from in the end. But even so, this is something that you do often for the fun of it.

If you are a rock star, you practice the same song frequently before a show, maybe changing some of the melody to make it fun for you and the audience. You do this because you love it, and you want to sound your best.

If you are a basketball player, you go to practice or watch films before a in order to get that confidence and winning feeling. That's a positive thing that makes you and your team better. If you overeat, or you choose that same kind of guy or a girl from the same kind of environment, most likely you will end up with the same result. Be aware of your habits and patterns and change them.

There are a lot of sacrifices that need to be made to change our habits or mindset. It's never, ever easy. But it's 100% possible, all you need to do is want to, have the belief that you can, and then be consistent about it.

The first move towards change for me was to change my environment. I moved from SoHo to the Upper West Side near the water, around families with kids, and old couples. It was the best move of my life! I cut myself out from the party scene and those kinds of areas, which is much easier to do when you are *away* from the scene! Do yourself a favor when you are trying to break a habit. If you want to quit smoking, don't hang out with smokers!

That was a game changer for me.

The physical part of it was easy, the mind part was challenging! At the same time, I soon realized as I was getting more and more relaxed and focused, that good things came to me very quickly. Suddenly, lots of new people came into my life. I expected to be alone for quite some time, but I wasn't! And the people that came into my life were people just right for the real me. I felt more open, smiled more, even my bad days were not that bad because things around me were changing in the right direction. Guys, taking these steps I'm showing you, for less than six months, I saw a change. And as I kept going, this change just got bigger and bigger. It was just so exciting that I had to share with you, with anyone who could benefit from it!

This brings me to the next step...

7. Slowing life down:

I know it sounds ridiculous, like how can you slow down life? Especially these days when we feel we are "on" 24/7. Well, to be honest when you can slow down your life, things are going faster. How? Well, you know that when you are doing something fun, time flies by right? It's like when you go to work and you are having fun during your shift and before you know it, you can go home! That's what happens when you slow down your life.

Slowing down your life means you can take step back and make the right choices for yourself so you can be happy and fulfilled. To return to the basketball analogy, think of a good player like MJ or Kobe or LeBron James, or Steph Curry. The reason why they are all so good, besides the skills they worked so hard to develop, is because they can enter a flow state where they are on fire, not missing a shot. It's as if the game slows down for them and allows them to see what's going on in a way that's different than the other players on the court. They can take that extra split second to make the best choice to win the game.

This is how we should all look at our lives; step back and identify what is good or bad for us, then change those habits, or whatever, that causes us to get the same results and change our mindset to get a better result.

By taking all these steps in your own way, in your own time, you will be able to figure things out, as I did.

This is my second book, and I'm doing even better than I was when I wrote my first. Waaaaay better, guys. I just want you guys to have the same feeling; it's awesome!

As I said, I made a decision that cost me many friends. The fact that those people are not in my life like they used to be allows me the opportunity to be who I am today. I have no regrets at all!

I have proven that I've made mistakes and forgiven myself (or my Monkey mind) that put me in this position. Yes, I had fun. Yes, it took me until the age of around thirty-seven to realize that it wasn't my way of life. And so, what?

Ray Kroc was fifty-two years old when he started to branch into McDonald's restaurants. He became a billionaire a few years later. He thought he was in the restaurant trade until he realized that he was in the real estate industry and was able to take over the ownership of the old McDonald's businesses. There are oh so many stories of people who became successful (or shall I say happy) in their later years.

It's never too late to change our habits, it's never too late to change our lives, or even something in our lives to improve ourselves or increase our daily fulfillment. If we don't feel better with ourselves, it affects others. When we improve ourselves, it's contagious. I have a friend who is a single mom. She is lost. She keeps making the same mistakes, hoping a good guy will come and rescue her from her life. It's hard to watch.

I ask her simple questions such as, "Are you happy?" And she is unable to answer, saying she doesn't know, which means she's not. So, I ask, "Does your child see you unhappy? Does he feel that too?"

She replied, "I don't know, I never thought about it!" She was so surprised by my question, but not in a bad way. It was giving her a new way of thinking about herself and how it affects her kid. I explained to her that I had the same issue with my mom, and in the end I "suffered" from the same issue as an adult. Her habits are truly what make her frustrated with her life, and this frustration over her life affects her kid. And the only way for a kid not to pick up the unhealthy habits of the parent, is for the parent to change their current habits to new ones. This example can be related to anyone in any given situation they are in now.

Changing our habits will allow us to slow down our lives in a way that we are going to be happy again. It will also make those around us happy. Emotions are contagious, the good and the bad.

The terms of the superego became well known in the late 19th and early 20th centuries through the psychoanalytic work of Sigmund Freud. The concepts themselves fit neatly into a traditional Jewish view of the human psyche. The idea that the part of the personality that consists of instinctual drives is considered present from birth. The superego, developed at a later stage of life, reflects the internalizing of moral rules inculcated by parents and teachers. The superego, which is intended to act as the conscious understanding of human nature, the *yetzer hara*, the evil impulse, is analogous to the Id, because it, too, is present from birth and, misdirected and unchecked, results in antisocial behavior. Analogous to the superego is the Monk inside of us. Our dear Monk...

It is the outcome of learning the moral rules of life that we have a Monk in our head.

Having internalized these rules of socially acceptable behavior, the conscious self can channel the urges of the *yetzer hara* into constructive activities, such as building a house, marrying and being faithful, having children, and modeling for them a life of study and good deeds, as well as conducting business affairs honestly.

In order for us to change our old habits we need to be aware of our habits firstly, then move from our comfort zone, and stop with the habits that are convenient to us. Small actions and small steps are the key to changing our old deep habits and moving from the Monkey mind to the light of our Monk.

In the Kabala, they talk about "cause and effect," the idea that at any moment in time, we are either the cause or the effect of our experience. Either we embrace our Divine Essence, our ability to embody the Creator's sharing light, our Monk, or we allow ourselves to be affected by all that is around us, within us, what people say about us, what people do, even our own emotions and reactions to life's challenges. We are simply reactive.

When we are simply the "effect," the reactive mode, it's always about the "me," i.e., what "I" got or didn't get, what "they" said about "me," how she wronged "me," and so on. And when we are the cause, we become facilitators for kindness, peace, and harmony. No matter what we do or what position we find ourselves in, if we have an aspect of sharing in our consciousness, then we can be the "cause," a motivating force for good in this world which I call the Monk.

The fact that we can do what we want and the option to ask for forgiveness gives me the impression that we were sent here because of our father's sins. When you feel overwhelmed by the worries, fears, and anxieties of the "me," stop for a minute and ask yourself where and why you feel like that. Then find a way to turn that consciousness around. See how you can take responsibility for how you react. See what you can do for others. Be the light in someone else's darkness. In doing so, you'll connect yourself with your Divine Essence, with your Monk, and with the realm of infinite possibility.

Life is all about taking responsibility for your actions, and reactions. Although every action in life is caused by you, we are talking about our own lives here. We should never care about someone else's business unless they ask for help. Yep, I've really learned that one! Yes, your friend may need guidance and you may desperately want to help them. But unless they are looking for a change, or ready to make a change, or are asking for help, our words will fall on deaf ears. They must be ready. But that aside, we certainly will not be able to help others or share our true love with others, if deep inside of us we are not happy with our own lives.

In Hebrew, one of the words for courage is "*ametz.*" "Be strong and courageous (*chazak ve'ematz*)," God tells Joshua. After Moses' death, Joshua needed strength and encouragement as the new leader of Israel. So, three times God encourages him with these words as he prepares to lead the nation into the Promised Land. The Hebrew word for strength, "*chazak*" can also mean courage. In fact, courage is derived from strength, and not just physical strength. The Bible is full of instances of moral, spiritual, intellectual, and social strength that God expects His children to practice and excel at in our journey from glory to glory. Let's look at a few of them.

- Be Strong and Courageous:

The Hebrew word for strength (*chazak*), begins with the deep guttural and throaty ch (*chet*) and ends with a strong letter k (*koof*), with the confident z (*zayin*) in between. It has the sound of strength and force! What kind of *chazak* does God expect us to have and when does He want us to use it? After all, there are a lot of risky situations we can walk into.

- How to Receive Divine Courage:

Sandwiched between two of the commands to be strong and courageous (*chazak v'ametz*), God explains to Joshua how to access that strength and courage.

"Keep this Book of the Law always on your lips; meditate on it day and night, so that you may be careful to do everything written in it. Then you will be prosperous

and successful. Do not be frightened or dismayed, for YHVH (the Lord) your God is with you wherever you go." The idea of praying for energy is very important. It's what gives us hope for a better future.

A form of the Ten Commandments is found in all religious books as well as many non-religious ones. We are the ones who can keep them or break them, therefore, the idea of keeping them can come out of love of the energy or the system of law that is built from them.

"If you love me, keep my commandments. And I will ask the Father, and He will give you another advocate to help you and be with you forever - the Spirit of truth. The world cannot accept Him, because it neither sees Him nor knows Him. But you know Him, for He lives with you and will be in you."

To keep them in the physical mind or physical act, in the end, all starts with the belief that if we follow those rules things will be better or get better. Instead of withdrawing, the disciples banded together and prayed for strength and boldness to continue sharing the love of God and healing. Although we may face criticism, rejection, and persecution we can rejoice in knowing we were courageous to take the step of taking responsibility and forgiving ourselves in order to move on quicker with our lives.

Our mind is the only reason why we can move on from our problems. Either you choose to hear the voice of the Monkey who has the ego mixed with emotions or we listen to our light, our Monk.

Breaking down your issues into small questions is key to giving you easy answers.

Now, the easy answers will come, but the actions of making those changes are hard. For example, you know there is an issue with a friend, their way of thinking or bringing you down or dragging you towards making bad choices. You know you need to cut them out of your life in order to change in the direction you need to go. But it's not easy.

If you can do it in one shot, that can be easier. Or, you can slowly stop connecting, or answering their calls or texts. For me, I find making excuses of why you can't meet with them, is quite draining and difficult. I prefer to just block. It's simpler and easier for me.

8. Don't expect:

I've stopped expecting anything from life. Really! And this is not borne out of negativity —I'm a lot happier! It's a mindset. I decided that expectations from people or myself can lead to unnecessary stress in life. Although some people can be fueled by the idea of expectations, most of us suffer as a result. I see expectation as a key to disappointment in every aspect of life. If you are not strong enough, expectations can mentally drain you with negative thoughts. Therefore, I stop expecting anything from anyone, even from myself.

If I want something to be done or changed, I do it. For example, now, when it comes to hiring people or asking for help from someone, it can take time. I have learned that I need to be there to direct them, to help them, and to catch any issues early on to see if we are wasting each other's time. The fact I don't expect anything from a new hire/or help, makes my life easier to solve issues that come up along the way, rather than getting frustrated when things don't meet my unrealistic expectations. Over time, you build trust, so in the end, the job will get done without you needing to be involved or expecting anything.

This step will not work, however, if you feel sure that things will get better no matter what the universe brings you

> "You will have bad times, but they will always wake you up to the stuff you weren't paying attention to." -
> **Robin Williams**

along the way. This step will not work if you don't see "bad" struggles as good things, as part of your healing or shaping, or for a better version of yourself. If you want to get better at something you need to understand your mistakes along the way. Again, it comes down to awareness.

If you keep getting the same bad results you learn and change something in order to gain a different result. I know bad things, and unfortunate situations can't always be good, but 95% of the time you can find the good inside the bad to improve yourself or your body. Either way, it will change your perspective of life if you see it that way, and for the better. How can it not?

"Darkness cannot drive out darkness, only light can do that. Hate cannot drive hate, only love can do that."
- **Martin Luther King**

So, if you want those steps to work you need to want this more than ever. If you decide to use my steps or find your own routine similar to mine, it will only work if:

- You don't rush each step
- You believe in yourself
- Most importantly: YOU WANT THIS, AND YOU ARE DOING THIS FROM A LOVING and HAPPY PLACE.

Otherwise, you can toss this book away! (Well, as long as you toss it towards someone else – don't toss it in the trash! Ha-ha!)

- If you expect something it will not work, if you come from a point of simply giving it a try or giving it 99% chance - it will not work.
- It will work if you want it to work!
- It will work if you believe it will work!

- It will work if you are doing it for yourself and for the love of yourself, not because I said so, or someone else said so.
- It will work because you want a change.

I can tell you this 100% worked as soon as I changed my mindset, not expecting it to work but believing it will, understanding that it can take time, understanding there can be some setbacks or bad days. Understand that if you want things to change *you* need to change.

I took my time, I took some space, I was scared but I knew I could be alone for a few months or years, whatever it took until I got to a more comfortable place. You will be surprised how well you cope. I have a chatterbox friend who went on a ten-day silent meditation retreat. No phones, nothing. How did she go? She aced it. She did better than she expected as is so often the case.

It wasn't easy for me, it wasn't easier for her, at first. But I got used to it, and when everything started to feel right again, then everything just started to come to me instead of me looking for them. I wasn't lost and alone, I was surrounded by people who truly cared.

> *"I think the saddest people always try their hardest to make people happy. Because they know what it's like to feel absolutely worthless and they don't want anybody else to feel like that."* -
> **Robin Williams**

I've now been living my dream for the past two years, and

not even realizing it! Have I mentioned awareness?! The difference between those two years and the rest of my life was the fact that I got to be aware of what my dream life was.

It wasn't about money or fame; it was about stability which I didn't have as a kid. You see, our past and especially our childhood reflects on our lives in a very powerful way.

Most of us don't even realize it, thinking, they won't be like our mom or dad. But as you know by now, (and as you age, it becomes more apparent), as we grow, we adopt a lot of habits that have stuck from our childhood habits, or our parent's habits, catching those habits early on and crushing them is hard, unless early on you go to a shrink.

I didn't go to a shrink, because for me, a shrink can't give me the resurrection I need if I can't be open about it. Not to mention it's expensive! All my life I was pretty closed off. I kept my feelings to myself and didn't feel ready to share the full story of my life.

In a way, it was a mistake, as I lost a lot of time finding myself, or finding my place and purpose in this world. I was juggling various opportunities, which was all good - we need to experience many different things in life. But the fear of losing the habit of living in a way that I was scared to lose something ended up making me lose everything! Cruel, huh? But that is what happens. I lived my life listening to the Monkey — "you'll lose her," "you're not good enough," etc. What you listen to, what you focus on, gets bigger.

As time passed, I was able to learn what was my biggest mistake of all! One word: naïve Being naïve is like being blind to what's really going on thinking or saying things such as:

- It will never happen to me.
- It will go away.
- It is just a matter of time, soon everything will be back to normal.

Unfortunately, it doesn't work that way. Just ask the six million Jews who didn't make it or those who did survive the holocaust. One of the biggest mistakes of the Jews was thinking that those new laws that came about, would go away. I mean, the rules were crazy! How could they possibly last?

There is a documentary on Netflix by Steven Spielberg about the Hungarian Jews who were living in small villages.

They all shared the same story about how everything was great. They were happy, life was good, and they lived in a beautiful area. Most importantly they had a good connection with their neighbors who shared their day-to-day lives at work, school, socially, and holidays. None of them ever thought their so-called neighbors would have anything bad to say about them. That is, until the day Hitler took over Hungary and they had to evacuate their homes. One of them reported that as they were outside, their neighbors called to them, "It's about time they took you from here!" She described how she was in shock seeing and hearing those words from her neighbors and supposed friends.

Their Hungarian naivety didn't end there. When the Jews were told, they were going to a better place, where they could all live among their own people, they were taken to train stations. Again, they were naïve when they were told that the passenger train was full of people, therefore they needed to take the industrial trains, where there was no light, air, water, or food.

You might think, "How could they be so naïve?" Well, I don't think anyone could imagine the atrocities that awaited them, especially those who liked to believe the best in people, the best in human nature. Only when the door to the train was locked, did they realize that it was all a lie. Can you imagine?

It was that kind of naïve thinking that if one keeps on going in an unhappy situation without making any changes, (to our habits or being aware of our reality) things will get better on their own. This is the Monkey's mind way of thinking, staying in the dark, lacking awareness, ignoring the signs, thinking things will get better when the opposite keeps happening.

One becomes comfortable with being unhappy, too. We can tend to think this is who we are, and this is normal, but it's not. My friends, it's just NOT.

Let's finish by going back to the Lion King; if we can understand the circle of life, we will be able to define ourselves. The bad or the good. It's really very simple, there is a lot of back and forth between scientists and the Book of God, as to where do we really come from?

The Book of God fashions Adam from dust and places him in the Garden of Eden.

Scientists say we originate from animals; studies showing that some of those animals that survived the "Big Bang" millions of years ago have the same blood cells as the human body.

I don't disagree with either approach, whether there is proof or not. I neither believe, nor disbelieve. It just proves my point that there are two different options to live our lives. There's the Monkey's way; those who choose to hunt, kill, feed their ego and greed, who seek attention, who are naïve and fearful. And there's the Monk's way; those who choose to love, nurture, who are aware, who give, who seek peace, fulfillment, who are wise and brave.

I want to end this book with a story.

On June 12, 2021, a European soccer player, Christian Eriksen, collapsed suddenly in the middle of a game. The game was Denmark vs. Finland. It was the second game of the tournament with millions of international viewers. What was supposed to be an exciting game, full of action, roars, and cheers, became silent for fifteen minutes. For those watching from the stadium and those watching from home, those fifteen minutes felt like an hour. They all watched the distraught faces on the TV of the players on the field watching the scene in horror. The viewers had no idea what was going on and it did not look good. The players created a shield to cover the accident from the cameras, while the medic was trying to bring him back to life. It was excruciating to watch. It was especially hard to witness his wife rushing onto the pitch, being held by the Denmark goalkeeper Kasper Schmeichel.

What struck me the most was everyone holding their hands in the universal sign of prayer, asking God to bring him back to life. This unfortunate situation united everyone in the world to do one thing: pray.

I'm sharing this story with you because for a moment we saw the power of prayer coming into effect in a matter of minutes! Those fifteen minutes were long and terrifying for everyone, especially his family. Why am I sharing this with you? Good question, I'm glad you asked!

For some reason, we all become united during bad circumstances. When I say "united" I mean we can be united on our own level, or a world level.

For example, when Covid-19 started to affect the world in a way that the world had to shut down, we all tried desperately to find a way to survive and find a vaccine. When an African American gets killed by a cop, we all want to go to the street, share our voices, and demand change. When someone overdoses or gets cancer and can come back and survive, we suddenly start to listen to our bodies. Basically, we get a wake-up call.

My question to you is, why do we need to witness or experience those Monkeyish events to make us change our lives? Why can't we just change ourselves because it's the right thing to do? Or is it a better way to live our lives because we know it will make us, and the people around us happier? We don't need these wake-up calls! Wake up now, my friends. Listen to your Monk, now.

Remember that your struggles have made you who you are today, the good and the not-so-good. But the good is a gift, you've got to use it. Maybe the gift will be a gift to share your story and help others? Maybe the gift is to work in an industry where your experiences and insights make a difference in countless ways.

Awareness and understanding of the Monkey's mind vs the Monk's light will take you where you want to go. If you choose to believe in the more spiritual side of the human race, you are choosing to be aware, kind, loving, helpful, grateful, thankful, respectful, and happy. There is no reason to fear anything. Go on and grab life, listen to your dear Monk.

Printed in the USA
CPSIA information can be obtained
at www.ICGtesting.com
JSHW070239110823
46354JS00008B/40

9 781524 318468